What people are saying ab...

"Dan Johnston provides sound approa[ch]... [pr]oblems with the compassion and understanding of a[n e]xperienced therapist."
~ W. Douglas Skelton, M.D., Senior Vice President for Health Affairs, Mercer University.

"Cogent, concise proverbs to help us lay claim to our own lives. Dr. Johnston shows us clear, simple ways to move beyond projection, blame, and familiar misery. Words of wisdom condensed."
~ Fr. Dan Edwards, Co-director of Omega Point, Author of *A Study Guide to Prayer Book Spirituality.*

"Everyone can benefit from the insights in *Lessons for Living.* In it, Dan Johnston gives us a down-to-earth guide to a happier, healthier life."
~ Oby Brown, Features Editor, *The Macon Telegraph.*

"Dan Johnston helps us transform the challenges and stresses of today into possibilities for tomorrow. His practical experience and optimistic outlook come to life for the reader."
~ Don Faulk, President, CEO, Central Georgia Health Systems.

What people are saying about *Lessons for Living:*

Lessons for Living offers wide-ranging, practical advice that highlights the importance of attitude and action in meeting the challenges of daily life.
~ Perry Buffington, Ph.D., Author of *Cheap Psychological Tricks.*

"The gift of *Lessons for Living* is a clear and potent guidance for joyful living. This unique and informative book has lessons for all of us. If you want to have a positive thought about yourself today or build a positive relationship for your future, read any of these 70 lessons."
~ Sylvia Shellenberger, Ph.D., Psychologist and Professor, Mercer University School of Medicine.

"Dan Johnston is able to communicate with clarity and simplicity on a subject as complex as coping with life's problems. Read, enjoy, and learn."
~ Ray H. McCard, M.D., President of The Psychiatric Center and Director of The Coliseum Psychiatric Center, Macon, Georgia.

Lessons for Living

Lessons for Living

Simple Solutions
for Life's Problems

Daniel H. Johnston, Ph.D.

Dagali Press
5663 Taylor Terrace
Macon, Georgia 31210

Dagali Press, 5663 Taylor Terrace, Macon, Georgia 31210
Phone: (478) 471-1008   E-mail: dagalipress@lessons4living.com

FIRST EDITION
First Printing, 2001

Library of Congress Control Number: 2001118036
ISBN: 0-9712165-0-9

Permissions: Portia Nelson's poem, *An Autobiography in Five Short
Chapters,* is used by permission of Beyond Words Publishing, Inc.

Cover design by John Powell, Panaprint
Cover photo by Dan Johnston

Disclaimer

The purpose of this book is to educate and entertain. The author will have no
liability or responsibility to any person(s) or entity with respect to any alleged
loss or damage caused either directly or indirectly by information contained in
the book. Readers should consult a health-care professional if they have questions regarding the information included in this book especially as it relates to
individual concerns regarding mental, emotional, and physical health.

Publisher's Cataloging-in-Publication
(*Provided by Quality Books,Inc*)

Johnston, Daniel H.
      Lessons for living : simple solutions for life's
      problems / Daniel H. Johnston. -- 1st ed.
      p. cm.
      Includes bibliographical references.
      ISBN 0-9712165-0-9

      1. Self-actualization (Psychology) 2. Success--
Psychological aspects. I. Title

      BF637.S8J64 2001   158.1
                        QBI01-700767

*To Grace Johnston and Howard Johnston
for guiding me with love.*

Table of Contents

Part Three: Lessons for Growing 132

Acknowledgments

I want to acknowledge the people who played a role in shaping this book. First, I would like to thank the many patients and clients I have counseled over the years. They helped me learn and refine many of the lessons offered here. In addition, I give thanks to my friends who read various drafts of the manuscript and offered not only their encouragement, but also the willingness to tell the truth with helpful criticism. Thanks go to Yvonne Elkins, Niki Collins-Queen, Jane Self, Alan Rumph, Dodie Cantrell, and Perry Buffington.

Richard Goudeau is deeply appreciated for serving as my editor. Not only was he thorough, but he was also kind and patient.

Special thanks go to my wife, Gail Johnston, who taught me the strength of love; to my daughter, Lisa Johnston, who taught me that life should be fun; and to my son, Kipp Howe, who taught me the power of forgiveness.

The thought manifests as the word;
The word manifests as the deed;
The deed develops into habit;
And habit hardens into character.

So watch the thought and its ways with care,
And let it spring from love;
Born out of concern for all beings.

As the shadow follows the body.
As we think, so we become.

~ Buddha from the Dhammapada

Introduction

Awakening Moments

A mind once stretched by a new idea can never go back to its original dimensions.

~ Oliver Wendell Holmes

Where in your life are you today? Are you comfortable, or are you comfortably miserable? What lesson is life teaching you today? Can you hear the message?

Most people do not hear the messages or see the lessons. Awakening moments pass them by. It may be that the lesson is so obvious that it is overlooked. The harried, rude clerk at the grocery store may be your teacher today, but you are so focused on what she/he did that you missed what you did. By contrast, the lesson may be so profound that it shakes you to your core, and you lose perspective. Being fired from a job may so totally disrupt your life that chances for growth are overlooked and a collapse into despair occurs.

Some people do glimpse the lesson but are so stuck in a position of wanting life to change—*while they remain the same*—that they do nothing. Life is trying to wake all of us to the fact that we are responsible for our own changing. To change we must act, and to act we must see the possibility of real choice and be willing to take responsibility.

Each day tries to teach us something. Each day offers awakening moments. An awakening moment is an instant of clarity in which new insight is gained. It is a moment in which "reality" is clearly seen, options are presented to us, and choices can be made. To say that reality is clearly seen means we see what is before us just as it is. We see the present moment stripped of the hopes or fears we project into it. We see the psychological reality we are creating and realize that it could be different. We see "what is" and not just what we bring to it. It may be a pleasant surprise or a rude shock, but it is reality—a reality that wakes us up if we glimpse it.

However, for the awakening moment to be useful, we must grasp it and perceive its meaning. Once understood, it brings a new awareness and the experience of life is viewed differently. New opportunities open up, and changes in patterns of thought, emotion, and behavior occur. Such an awakening allows the possibility of growth to new levels of psychological and spiritual maturity.

Awakening moments can be ordinary—as ordinary as a rainy day. I have a photograph of an awakening moment. It was taken on a day that started sunny but soon turned to rain. During a bus ride from Salisbury, England, to the ancient stone formations at Stonehenge, a downpour occurred. I grumbled to myself and to my wife about how the rain would ruin this long-awaited trip. Later, walking around Stonehenge in the cold, wet mist, I was disappointed with the day and continued to grumble. Suddenly the rain stopped. For a few glorious moments the sun broke through the clouds, and a rainbow appeared. My photograph of a rainbow over Stonehenge captured this awakening moment.

That rainy day, and especially that moment, became the highlight of my two-week trip to England. It also opened me to a new attitude. Without the rain, I would not have found the rainbow. This simple truth is very profound when it becomes a lived experience. Grumbling about the immediate situation does not help. It only distracts from what is happening. We must be open to every moment— open to possibility. We never know what it will bring.

Opening Up

Opening to the moment can be difficult because in order to be open, we must be willing to change. In life, we become comfortably settled into routines that are not easily given up. Sometimes the comfortable routine is actually more of a comfortable misery, a misery that is familiar and whose depths we know. When life is comfortable, even comfortably miserable, it feels risky to change. It is easier to stay the same. Why jeopardize a state of comfort?

The problem is that if we stay comfortable long enough, we become stuck. Comfort that becomes a routine can turn into a rut. When a rut is deep enough, it becomes a grave, and we are covered over with the inertia of inaction. Life loses its vitality and meaning.

While it is difficult to change when we are comfortable, opening to change is less difficult when we are in distress. It is not that hard to change when we feel impelled to seek relief. Awakening moments often come out of broken moments that open us to new possibilities.

While we do not intentionally seek broken moments, life hands them to us anyway. Often they come our way because we were too comfortable too long, and lived out the comfortable pattern until it no longer worked. Had we been more mindful, given up comfort on purpose, and taken a chance, life may not have fallen apart.

Learning to seek change, even in the presence of comfort, can lead to a more meaningful life. The paradox is that learning to challenge our comfort zones may also keep life from falling apart. Being motivated to continually grow and develop enables us to challenge ourselves—to stay on the cutting edge of life. Being open to change, even in the midst of comfort, gives life vitality. Each day we must actively look for opportunities to grow. For a meaningful life, we must engage in the daily, intentional challenging of comfort. We must constantly push our limits to achieve our "personal best," much the way champion athletes in the pursuit of excellence seek to set new records.

The Challenge to Change

Do you want life to go better? Do you want to change today? Are you willing to work hard to improve your life? For nearly thirty years I have worked as a psychologist and these are questions I ask the people I counsel at the beginning of every session. They are just ordinary people with problems. Some are depressed; others are anxious or angry; some have addiction problems; some are struggling with a chronic illness. Family problems, marital conflict, and job stress may be involved. What I want to know from them is simply this: *Do you want to get better and are you willing to work at it?*

Most often the answer is "yes" and "no." "Yes" they want to get better, but "no" they really don't want to work at it. People often are looking for magic. They want some magic words, a magic pill, or even a magic wand. Those looking for magic words go from one counselor to another or from one self-help book to another and are always dissatisfied. Those who are looking for a magic pill hope their doctor can find the right medicine. They have tried everything and nothing seems to work for them. If their condition has worsened, it is always because their medicine has stopped working, and now they need a new prescription. Moreover, no one seems to know where to find the magic wand, so instead of looking for the wand there is sometimes a frantic search for the "magical person" (spouse, lover, guru) who can make life wonderful.

Magic *is* hard to find, but the absence of magic is not the primary problem. The fundamental difficulty in changing our lives is one of having to directly face issues of responsibility, choice, and action. To improve our lives, we must assess the situation, determine what we control, make a choice, and take action. We must create our own magic. If we want to change, we must take a chance. We must let go of where we are, so we can get to where we are going. This "letting go" is a scary prospect because we know and are familiar with the relative safety of where we are even if it is unpleasant at the moment.

Making a change is like leaping from the safety of one trapeze to another. There is a risky time during when you are in mid-air. Why would you attempt such a leap? What if you didn't make it? Perhaps you could just hold on, refuse to leap, and stay where it momentarily feels safe. Maybe you must leap because you cannot tolerate your present situation any longer. You leap out of a sense of desperation. You could be slowly losing your grip; so, you leap before you fall. Furthermore, you may be roughly shaken from the trapeze when a crisis arises and things cannot stay the same.

Whether you choose to change or have change thrust upon you, it helps to have a plan. It helps to have some sense of how life works and what can be done to regain balance and momentum.

Using Your Common Sense

In a psychiatric hospital where I once worked, patients stayed an average of four days. They brought intense problems with them, but received only four days of treatment. Before the days of managed health care, they may have stayed four weeks. While this may have been too long, four days is often too short. What can be done in four days?

People can be challenged to use their common sense. Common sense is just information that makes sense to us once we hear it. Common sense presents itself whenever we learn something and then think, "I knew that." True—we did know it. But we were not using the information. We had forgotten what we knew and needed a reminder. In the hospital setting, people needed reminders to explore their common sense, evaluate their situation, and then test out what they "knew" through action.

Common sense is obvious and self-evident, but only after we have seen it. Before that, we are often oblivious to its presence. Later, we wonder, "How could I have missed it?" Frequently, we miss the common sense solution because we do not want to see it. If we acknowledge common sense, then we face the frightening possibility of having to change. We are confronted with our responsibility for our life situation and must decide whether or not to act on what we now know. If we choose not to see the common sense solution, we may not have to change. We avoid responsibility, but we stay stuck.

Lessons for Living

This book is a series of "lessons for living." It consists of simple, practical essays on how you can make your life more liveable. Brief, to-the-point chapters provide insight into life's problems and suggest courses of action. Some lessons are a variation on a basic theme and present the same information from different viewpoints to aid better understanding. Each chapter can be read independently and used as a guide for daily change. Or, when read as a whole, the series of lessons provide a model for living a more joyful and meaningful life.

These lessons also serve as common sense reminders. They will help you remember what you know and challenge you to use it. Try out each lesson and see if it works for you. Your daily life is a laboratory for such experimentation and learning. Use each day as an experiment. Try something new and see what works. You will only know what works for you by testing it out for yourself.

❖❖❖❖

Part One:

Lessons for Remembering:
What Everyone Needs to Know

Part One of *Lessons for Living* focuses on responsibility, attitude, and choice. We must all learn the basic "facts of life." While we may resist this knowledge, we must come to understand that we are responsible for all of our life experience. Our responsibility comes as a direct consequence of the attitude we adopt and the choices we make. Before waking up to these "facts of life," we act as if life controls us. Afterwards, we know that we have control if we will do the hard work of assuming responsibility. The following chapters examine this "waking up" process through lessons on the challenge of changing, the rules for living, and the power of mind over matter.

❖❖❖❖

Lesson 1

The Rules for Living

Nothing is good or bad, but thinking makes it so.

~ Shakespeare

Examine the following statement. Is it true or false? *"You are responsible for all of your experiences of life."* Most people quickly say it is false, arguing that they don't cause everything that happens to them. This is certainly true. All kinds of things happen to you that you don't cause. However, the statement is absolutely true. You *are* responsible for *all* of your experiences of life.

Now, it is a bit of a trick. Notice that the statement says *of* life and not *in* life. You are not responsible for everything that happens to you, although you may often contribute to it. Many things will happen, both good and bad, over which you have no control—floods, tornadoes, and the fluctuations of the stock market. These events are your experiences *in* life. Your reactions to them are your experiences *of* life. You always control your experiences of life. This is exciting news. It means that you can take charge of your life.

Life has rules sometimes known as the "facts of life." These are not the "birds and bees" facts but the real facts about how life works. If you know the facts and the rules and follow them, life goes better. Here are the "facts."

Life appears to have two steps. Step One is *Life Acts* which simply means that something happens in life. Let's call it X—the unknown. Event X happens, and it can be anything. You might get married, get divorced, be fired, receive a promotion, or win the lottery. Once *Life Acts*—once something happens to you—it is your turn.

Step Two is *You React*. You react to whatever has happened with response Y. Y also represents the unknown because it is not certain what you will do. What is certain is that your response always includes some emotional reaction. You *feel* something—perhaps happiness, sadness, anger, or frustration. Your response also includes a behavioral reaction. You *do* something. You respond in some way, such as laughing, crying, or jumping for joy.

Viewed from a distance it appears that event X causes your reaction Y. If your boss criticizes your report, you might get angry, tear it up, and throw it into the wastebasket. Later, you tell someone, "My boss made me mad." Thus, it appears that life has two steps: *Life Acts* and *You React*. External events cause your responses.

In reality, however, life has three steps. Step One is *Life Acts.* Your boss criticizes your report. Step Two is *You Think*. You think about what happened and about what your boss said. You start thinking, "He is always picking on me. It's horrible. I can't stand it." And, Step Three—*You React.* Your emotional response is anger, and your action is to tear up the report and throw it away.

You have created your own negative reaction with what you have been telling yourself. You do have other choices. You could think, "Great, now I can correct the report before the staff meeting." Your reaction will be different as you feel a sense of relief and get busy with the corrections.

In between life's action and your reaction, something has to be done in order for you to have any reaction at all. After becoming aware of what has happened you must *think* about it. In thinking, you evaluate the event and create your response.

Once you become aware that something has happened, the Voice of Conscience speaks up and tells you what it means. The Voice of Conscience is that "little voice" that talks to you. You probably recognize it as the one that speaks up when you look in the mirror or get on the bathroom scale. It can say how wonderful you look or how out of shape you are. The Voice can be positive or negative.

This Voice of Conscience is simply you talking to *you*. It is you telling yourself about life. Your Voice of Conscience can talk you into a lot of trouble, or it can talk you into a positive outlook that changes your life experience.

Learn to listen to the Voice of Conscience, and catch it when it is talking nonsense. Catch it when it is being too critical and when it is too extreme. Catch yourself when you are making things worse than they are. Change the nature of your inner dialogue and life will go better. Control your reactions to life by monitoring your thinking. Learn to think realistically—without exaggeration—about life.

Life will give you enough trouble. Don't make things worse than they are. When driving to work, if someone suddenly pulls into your lane making you miss a turn, don't focus on what a jerk the other driver is. Don't tell yourself how it always happens to you. Don't rave and rant about the injustice of it all. Accept the reality of the inconvenience and keep driving. You will get to your destination, perhaps a few minutes late, but you will be in a better frame of mind and in a better mood.

Remember: *Life Acts*, and *You React*, but in between *You Think*. Choose your reaction by choosing *what* you think. Pay attention to your inner dialogue. How you talk to yourself is important. Be sure you are making sense. Take responsibility for your thinking. Always choose a realistic but positive point of view and make life go better.

❖❖❖❖

- ◆ Recall a recent event that upset you.
- ◆ How did you react?
- ◆ What were you telling yourself about the event?
- ◆ Was there another more positive point of view?
- ◆ Would it have changed your reaction?

Lesson 2

Comfortable Misery: Not Ready to Change

Misery no longer loves company. Nowadays it insists on it.
~ Russell Baker

A re you in a bad situation that you wish would just go away? Maybe it is the dull routine into which your life has fallen or the dead-end job that you have. Perhaps it is your small, cramped apartment. You are unhappy and frustrated and complain about how terrible it is, but you don't take action. You won't change. You feel stuck, and you are. You are caught in comfortable misery.

Comfortable misery is a situation that you don't like, but one to which you have grown accustomed. Think of a bad marriage that has gone on so long that both spouses have resigned themselves to it. Neither likes it, and both complain about it, but no one leaves. It is a habit and brings a sense of safety. Leaving might not only bring loneliness but also require demanding and risky changes. Perhaps it is better to just stay the same. Why take a chance?

Comfortable misery means you *are* miserable, but you are used to it. You know the limits and bounds of *this* misery, and also that you can tolerate a situation this bad because you do it every day. The problem is that trying to get out of comfortable misery is frightening. You could make a change, but then what? You're tempted by the hope that things could get better, but paralyzed by the fear that they could get worse. You wonder, "If it got worse, could I stand it?" You think, "If I change, I might create something even more miserable. I could be jumping from the frying pan into the fire. Maybe it's better to stay the way I am. At least I know I can tolerate it."

This type of thinking holds you back and keeps you stuck. While you are miserable, you are not miserable enough to change. How miserable do you have to get?

You can wait until your situation becomes a crisis, and you are impelled to act, but this isn't the best way to change. It is better to take responsibility and plan your action. Look around. What are your choices? What can you do? Be realistic about your resources and possible outcomes. Anticipate what might go wrong and be prepared for it. Accept the fact that you might be somewhat more uncomfortable as you go through the change process, but be optimistic and hold onto the expectation that things will improve.

Which is better—quick and intense or slow and steady? Think of a Band-Aid that you need to remove. Do you pull it off quickly to get it over with, or do you remove it slowly so as not to hurt yourself? Slow and steady can actually be more painful. Quick will also hurt, but it is soon over.

Quick is when you directly confront the misery of your alcohol abuse by choosing the difficult path of going into treatment rather than waiting to hit bottom. It is when you choose the discipline of joining the health club rather than continuing to complain about the difficulty of losing weight; it is when you break the misery of a bad relationship by packing your bags and leaving.

Comfortable misery gradually increases in intensity. Action is the best remedy for comfortable misery. It may be temporarily unpleasant, even difficult, as you change, but life can get much better when you are no longer stuck. You can jump out of the frying pan and over the fire. You can leap in to a new opportunity—a new possibility.

Remember: you have the power of choice. Take a chance. You only have your misery to lose.

❖❖❖❖

- ◆ Recall a past state of comfortable misery.
- ◆ How long did you stay in it?
- ◆ What did you do to get out of it?
- ◆ Are there current areas of your life in which you are comfortably miserable?
- ◆ What can you do today to give up comfortable misery?

Lesson 3

Being Unrealistically Unhappy: Too Miserable to Change

Life is full of misery, loneliness, and suffering—and it's all over much too soon.

~ Woody Allen

Most people's lives would improve if they could just learn to be realistically unhappy. To be realistically unhappy means to react to the negative events of life, such as divorce, losing a job, or failing at an important task, with an appropriate amount of distress. It is normal to be upset by these events—to a point. Being realistically unhappy helps you to accept the unfortunate events in life and gives you the motivation to move past them.

Not everyone accepts realistic unhappiness. They avoid it in one of two ways: denial or exaggeration. Those who deny their unhappiness pretend they don't have a problem (when they do) by saying things like, "I can stop drinking whenever I want." Or, "This job stress never bothers me." Denial is like sweeping the problem under the carpet. It only gets bigger when out of sight. It grows in the dark until it can no longer be ignored and becomes a crisis. It is better to directly face the issue and be realistic even if it makes you unhappy.

Some people avoid reality by exaggerating and making everything worse than it is. Whenever anything mildly unpleasant happens, they start thinking about how bad it is going to become and about all of the things that may go wrong. They reach out into the future of imagined bad possibilities and bring them back into the present moment. They begin living as if the worst case scenario is their new reality and become much unhappier than the actual event warrants. These people are "unrealistically unhappy" and create more trouble than they need.

For example, the loss of a job is a real problem. Most people would be distressed. Let's say that most people would be about 50 percent miserable, and let's call this normal.

Now, suppose you get a layoff notice and lose a job. You respond by becoming 50 percent miserable, but on the way home you start thinking. You tell yourself, "This is terrible. I bet that I will never get another good paying job. My spouse will be upset. My kids will be mad. My car will be repossessed. I will lose my home and wind up living on the street. This is terrible." By the time you arrive home, your misery may have doubled to 100 percent. Where did all this extra misery come from? You have created it from an imagined future of bad things that have not happened. You have made yourself unrealistically unhappy.

If, in a few days, none of these imagined bad things happen, and you get a lead on a job, you may rethink the situation. You may shrink your misery back down to 50 percent. You return to normal. Your life will have improved, but you still have a problem. You don't have a job. However, you are now *realistically* unhappy and can use this normal degree of unhappiness to motivate yourself into action.

Remember, when life gives you a problem, don't create more misery than you need. Learn to be realistically unhappy, and life will go better.

❖❖❖❖

- ◆ Are you currently unhappy?
- ◆ What happened to cause your unhappiness?
- ◆ Have you added to it?
- ◆ Is your unhappiness realistic or not?
- ◆ Can you rethink your situation and improve your life?

Lesson 4

Being in Crisis: Forced to Change

Watch out for emergencies. They are your big chance.

~ Fritz Reiner

Have you ever been caught up in a crisis? Have you ever had life suddenly fall apart? Perhaps you were overwhelmed by the loss of a job or the breakup of a relationship. Maybe it was just a minor event, but it was the straw that broke the camel's back; suddenly, you were in a crisis.

While such times can be very upsetting, understanding the true nature of a crisis can help you get through them. In Chinese, the meaning of a crisis is very well expressed. Writing the word "crisis" in Chinese requires two characters—one represents danger and the other opportunity. Translated from Chinese, a crisis is a "dangerous opportunity."

What do you usually see in a crisis? Danger or opportunity? Most of us quickly perceive danger and overlook the opportunity. We are naturally "danger people." Evolutionary history dictates that this is true. Survival of the species depends upon our recognizing and avoiding situations or events that might injure or kill us. When something changes in our environment, we immediately look to see how it might harm us. It pays to be vigilant and scan the environment for danger.

Being a person who sees opportunity goes against this natural instinct. Indeed, the opportunity may be well hidden. Our fundamental problem in coping with a crisis is that typically, after looking for the danger, we forget to look for the opportunity.

Becoming an Opportunity Person is hard work. It requires an intentional shift of your mindset—a change of attitude. This change of attitude often occurs only after successfully weathering several crises. Many people report that it was actually a crisis that caused them to perceive the possibility of making a much-needed change. Living through a hard time challenges people to grow in ways that often make them more mature and open them to new possibilities.

Community crises provide an example. In times of natural disaster—a flood, tornado, earthquake—people reach out to each other. They let go of self-centered interests and become connected in ways that strengthen them. Hidden in the danger of the disaster is the opportunity for the growth of empathy and caring which enables a true sense of community to develop and endure.

An individual crisis can also be life changing through hidden opportunity. Suppose you lose a job that you don't like. Maybe you had been thinking of leaving, but it was too scary to take the needed action. Now the company is downsizing and you are unemployed. Life has given you an opportunity to take a chance. You are in a crisis with both danger and opportunity. While one real danger is financial hardship, the deeper and more important danger is that you might put life back together just the way it was. You might plead to get your job back, and once again become stuck in a bad situation. You would be back in the job that you did not like, and soon you would be complaining again.

Instead, after weighing all the options, you could take a risk and use the crisis as an opportunity to make needed changes. You could return to school and through struggle and hard work advance to your goal: a more fulfilling career. You will arrive where you wanted to be because you seized the opportunity created by a crisis. Danger was present, but you chose to capitalize on the opportunity—the result was personal growth.

The next time a crisis enters your life, be sure to assess the danger and take any appropriate action. But remember to also look for the opportunity. What options do you have? What new directions are open to you? Become an Opportunity Person. Choose the Opportunity Attitude and your life will go better.

❖❖❖❖

- ◆ What was your most recent crisis?
- ◆ What was the danger and what was the opportunity?
- ◆ Did you capitalize upon the opportunity?
- ◆ If so, how did you do it?
- ◆ If not, what can you do now?

Lesson 5

Being Responsible: Choosing to Change

You must take personal responsibility. You cannot change the circumstances, the seasons, or the wind, but you can change yourself. That is something you have charge of.

~ Jim Rohn

There is a good chance that I know the person who causes most of your trouble. You probably know this person as well. Most likely, it is *you*. You are responsible for the choices and actions that have put you in your present circumstances. Like it or not, you *are* responsible, and this is good news. It is good news because you can change the things for which you are responsible. You can make your life go better.

However, it is human nature to try and avoid responsibility by passing it to someone else. We pass the responsibility through blame. We say, "It's not my fault. He/she made me do it." Or, "If my mother had treated me better, I wouldn't be this way." It may be as common and everyday as dropping and breaking a coffee cup. If asked what happened we say, "It slipped." Not, "I dropped it." Saying "it slipped" means that the cup is responsible for its own falling. We don't just admit we did it. We pass the blame. We try to get out of responsibility.

Avoiding responsibility has a long history, all the way back to Adam and Eve. After forbidding that the "apple" be eaten, God was suspicious and asked Adam if he had tasted the fruit. What did Adam do? He blamed Eve for giving it to him. When God asked Eve about this, she blamed the Snake for deceiving her. Had the Snake been asked the same question, the blame would surely have been passed again, perhaps back to God.

This archetypal story shows how reluctant we are to acknowledge our mistakes and say, "Yes I did it. I'm responsible." The problem arising from this reluctance is that if you don't like what is happening in your life but are not responsible for it, you can't change it. If you are not responsible, you have no control or influence. If you are not responsible, then someone else must be. You are a victim, and others are in control of your life. If your life is to get better, then *they*—the others—must change. So, you get busy trying to make *them* be just the way you want *them* to be so you can be okay. Changing others so that your life can improve is not an effective plan.

A better life strategy is for you to claim your responsibility and change the situation yourself. Don't wait on others to change and don't try to change them. If you can name and claim a problem, you can change it. Naming and claiming your responsibility gives you control.

To be responsible is to be "response-able"—able to make a response, able to do something. Responsibility leads to action. When you accept responsibility, you are in charge. You can change your thinking and attitude and plan a course of action. You can change your behavior and accept and deal with your emotions. You can claim your power and make a difference because you are willing to say, "I *am* responsible." Learn to claim and exercise your responsibility and life will improve.

❖❖❖❖

- Are there areas of your life in which you feel like a victim and blame others for your circumstances?
- Carefully evaluate these situations to determine what you do control.
- Take responsibility and change what you can.

Lesson 6

Simple Solutions: Easily Understood, Not Easily Done

Everything should be made as simple as possible, but not one bit simpler.

~ Albert Einstein

Most problems we face in life have a simple solution. Think about it. Frequently when you confront a problem, you already know what to do or could easily find out. You don't need a complex answer.

For example, the solution to the problem of losing weight is simple. You only need to know two things and almost everyone knows them. Eat less and exercise more. What could be simpler?

Yet if you have ever tried this simple solution for losing weight, you probably found it very difficult to do. Simple and easy are not the same. Simple means easily understood, not easily done.

Life actually has a lot of simple solutions. Do you need to stop smoking? It is simple. Don't light up again. Do you need more exercise? Also simple: always climb the stairs. Need to relax? Sit down and take a deep breath.

Changing is the key to solving these life problems. And the real difficulty of change is not that we don't know what to do, but that we can't seem to do what we should. Understanding alone is not sufficient. The doing is the hard part, and that is where discipline comes in. It is not that easy to, as one Nike commercial admonishes, "Just do it."

In order to change, what is required is intentional daily effort. Wake one morning, focus on your goal, and begin the work of change. Work at it all day long, every day, until the goal is reached.

Such effort must be done mindfully. You must observe yourself in the process, and when you wander away from the task (which you will), just bring yourself back and begin again. If you wander away and return enough times, you will eventually reach your goal.

This process works much like an airplane's autopilot. The autopilot is programmed toward a destination. As the plane flies it wanders off course to the right, but soon self-corrects and comes back on course only to wander too far to the left. Once again, it self-corrects, but overcorrects. Through this process of continually returning to the goal, the plane eventually arrives at its destination even though it may have been off course 90% of the time. You too can reach your goal, even if you are frequently off course. Just monitor yourself and self-correct.

Solving life's problems requires effort plus self-correction. It is important to note that self-correction is not self-criticism. Self-correction uses information to help you refocus and begin again. Self-criticism uses information to rob you of energy and stop the process of change.

The next time that you stray from your goal and eat a doughnut or light up a cigarette, don't fall into negative self-criticism. It will only distract and discourage you. Simply refocus on the goal and begin again. Begin enough times and you will succeed.

Also, when facing any problem in life, always check to see if the solution is *simple*. See if you already know what to do. If you do, then you can *"Just do it."*

❖❖❖❖

- ◆ Identify one of your current problems.
- ◆ Does it have a simple solution?
- ◆ Do you already know what to do?
- ◆ If so, "Just do it."
- ◆ How can you begin this process? What is the first step?
- ◆ Monitor your progress with self-correction.

Lesson 7

Watching Your Language

He can who thinks he can, and he can't who thinks he can't.
This is an inexorable, indisputable law.

~ Henry Ford

Some words create problems for us. Especially when we use them without thinking about their true meaning. The way we think and the words we use determine our reactions to life. Life acts, and we react, but in between we think. Watch out for what you think. You may be creating more trouble than you need.

Take the word "can't" for example. Have you ever said to yourself, "I can't?" As in, "I can't do it." What did you mean? What is it that you can't do? Right now think of something you *can't* do. People often say something like, "I can't lose weight." "I can't stop smoking." Or, "I can't forgive." None of these statements are true.

What did you think of? What is it that you can't do? Most likely what you thought of isn't true either. You see "can't" means that it cannot be done. If it can't be done, then it is impossible. So, you can't fly like a bird, walk through walls, or run a two-minute mile. All of these statements are true.

Most often when we say we can't do something, we are using the wrong word. "Can't" is not the right word. *Won't* is the right word. It is not "I can't," but "I won't." Won't means will not. It means, "I choose not to."

If we change our words our statements to ourselves sound different. They become, "I won't lose weight, stop smoking, or forgive." All of these options are actually possible; we just choose not to do them.

Most of us do not like this change of words from "can't" to "won't" because it confronts us with our responsibility for not taking action. After all, if you say you can't do it, you let yourself off the hook. When you say you can't, you give yourself permission not to make the effort.

- If you can't lose weight—don't try.
- If you can't stop smoking—give up.
- If you can't forgive—keep holding a grudge.

You get to give up before you start. You allow yourself to be stuck with a problem of your own choosing.

Learn to take responsibility for your words and choices. Intentionally make choices. It is all right to decide not to do something. Just take responsibility for your decision. You may choose not to lose weight, stop smoking, or forgive. That's okay. Make the choice not to do it. Just don't convince yourself it is impossible to do. Don't give yourself the easy way out. Taking responsibility for your thoughts and actions puts you in control of yourself, rather than having you feel controlled by habits, emotions, and circumstances.

Challenge yourself to make choices. Listen for the word "can't." When you hear yourself saying it, call time-out. Try out the word "won't" and see if it fits better. If you don't like it when you say it, "won't" is probably the right word. It challenges you to make a conscious choice and to exercise responsibility.

Pay attention to the words you use. You can talk yourself into more trouble than you need. Change your language, and your life may begin to go better.

❖❖❖❖

- Listen to yourself today and see if you can catch yourself saying some of these other problem words such as, "I should…," " I always…," or "I never…."
- How can these phrases create problems for you?
- What other problem words can you identify?

Lesson 8

Getting Off Your "But"

Everything you want is out there waiting for you to ask.
Everything you want also wants you. But you have to take
action to get it.

~ Jack Canfield

Have people ever played this game with you? They come with a problem asking what they should do. It might involve a family situation, financial concerns, or a job conflict. No matter what advice you give, no matter how hard you try to help, they always have the same response. You make a suggestion, and they say, "Yes, but... "

Perhaps they want to lose weight. You advise, "Exercise more." You hear, "Yes, I could, but running always hurts my knees." Well, you say, "Try riding a bike." They respond, "Yes, I could, but first I would have to buy one, and then I have no place to store it." "How about joining a gym?" "Yes, I could do that, but you know it just costs so much. Besides, I really hate exercising with all those thin people." On and on and on it goes, further and further into inaction. Eventually, you give up, and so do they.

Are you familiar with this game? The game of "Yes, but." Maybe you have even played it a time or two yourself. It is a way of staying the same and avoiding responsibility. It is a way of avoiding the hard and sometimes unpleasant work of changing. If you always play the game of "Yes, but," not only will you frustrate those around you, but you will stay stuck with your problems.

If "Yes, but" happens to be one of your favorite games, you will have to learn to get off your "but" if you want to make progress. Eliminate the word "but" from your replies to advice and suggestions. Instead, learn to say, "Thank you." Make sure that your response to any advice is always, "Yes, thank you." You don't have to say anything more. Just don't immediately rule out possibilities with an automatic, "Yes, but." Don't look for an easy excuse for not changing. Challenge yourself to explore all the options available to you.

Saying, "Yes, thank you" does not commit you to action. It just allows you to consider the option that is offered. You get to think it over and evaluate the practicality of it. Maybe you *have* tried the suggestion before, and it did not work *then*. However, what about *now*? Maybe things have changed, and it will work if you try again. Even if you decide it won't work, that is all right. At least you considered it.

Give up playing the "Yes, but" game and in the future you may find yourself saying, "Yes, thank you. Exercise may help, and I will consider a bike. Joining the gym could even be fun. Those skinny people will certainly motivate me."

Remember, you must get off your "but" if you want life to go better.

❖❖❖❖

◆ Learn to listen for yourself saying, "Yes, but...."
◆ Challenge yourself each time you say it.
◆ Make yourself give up excuses.

Lesson 9

Creating Your Own Reality

We are what we think. All that we are arises with our thoughts.
With our thoughts, we make our world.

~ Buddha

The first time it was suggested to me that I created my reality, I thought it was absurd. I didn't understand. I knew that I did not create the trees and flowers, or the sun and the rain, or this chair on which I am sitting. I don't create physical reality.

Physical reality, however, was not the level of reality that was meant. We have our physical reality and our psychological reality. I do create my psychological reality, and you create yours. This is good news because if we create it, we can change it.

Many different things happen to us in life, and often we have no control over them. Nonetheless, once an event happens, we always begin thinking about it. Thoughts begin to flow. They are either positive or negative. We are thinking either, "This is terrible." Or, "This is great." There may be a flood of thoughts—positive or negative. If the thoughts are negative, then the danger is that they may become a mental snowball rolling downhill, picking up speed and momentum, and sometimes crashing into things with disastrous effects.

It is with the act of thinking that we create our reality—our psychological reality, and this is where we all live. We live in our minds with the reality we create. Whenever anything happens to us, we choose what we think about it. Sometimes the thoughts are habitual and happen so quickly that it seems that there was no thought at all. But, if you slow down and catch yourself in action, you will see that you always tell yourself something. Either, "This is good," or "This is bad."

Knowing that you do this, you can begin to choose what to say to yourself, and learn to select more realistic and positive thoughts.

For example, lose a job and you could tell yourself, "It's hopeless. I'll never work again." Or, "It's tough, but I'll get through it." If a relationship has broken up you could think, "I'm just a loser. No one will ever love me." Or, "Just because one person doesn't love me, it does not mean no one will." When you make a mistake, don't call yourself "stupid" but accept mistakes as a normal part of life.

Consistently focus on the more positive viewpoint and you will be creating a better reality for yourself—a better psychological reality. With an improved psychological reality or attitude your experience of life will also improve. You will have a better outlook. You will feel a sense of acceptance—even over things you can't control.

Remember, you always get to choose your point of view over whatever life hands you. Be sure you choose the best viewpoint you can. Always create a good reality for yourself.

❖❖❖❖

- How have you created your reality today?
- Recall a minor event, such as a delay in traffic or *another* telemarketer's call.
- What kind of reality did you create for yourself?
- Was it positive or negative?
- Was it the reality that you desired?
- Can you change it now?

Lesson 10

Choose a New Attitude Each Day

The greatest discovery of my generation is that human beings can alter their lives by altering their attitudes of mind.

~ William James

Do you have an attitude today? Of course you do. You are awake, and you have been thinking. Each morning when you awake, you choose an attitude, and you have a chance to choose a new, and perhaps a better, attitude than you had the day before. Or, you may just recycle the same old negative attitude from last week, last month, or last year.

This is how attitude works. Each morning when you wake up there is a voice that begins talking to you. It may not speak up right away. It might wait until you get out of bed, walk into the bathroom, and look in the mirror. Then you hear, "Wow! You look great. You are such a slim, trim, beautiful person. You have such enthusiasm. Everyone likes you. What a fantastic day." Is this the voice you heard today? No?

Well, this voice is sometimes grumpy. You look in the mirror and hear something like, "You look terrible. Your hair is a mess. You've gained ten pounds, and that job you've got is going to kill you one day. Just get back in the bed. Don't get up." Do you recognize this voice? Did you hear it this morning?

One of these voices is trying to talk you into a good day, and the other is taking you down the road toward a bad day. Now, consider this. Just who is doing all this talking? Who is this voice? Well, of course, it is you. It is *you* talking to you. This is your Voice of Conscience telling you how life is going. It is busy creating an attitude—an outlook on life. Be careful what you say to yourself. If you go too far down the path toward a bad attitude day, you may not be able to turn around. You will just have to wait until the next day and try again.

Starting a day with a bad attitude is like rolling that familiar snowball of negative thinking downhill once again. It starts getting bigger and bigger and picks up speed. Soon it is out of control and crashing into everything in its path.

Don't let this happen to you. Learn to listen to your Voice of Conscience and monitor what it says. Don't just recycle a bad day. Intentionally choose a more positive outlook. Dispute the negative comments. Say, "No, I don't look terrible. My hair will look fine once I style it. I am exercising everyday and actually lost five pounds. My job is difficult, but I will make the best of it until I find the one I want." This is a more realistic dialogue and gives you a head start on a good attitude day.

Charles Swindoll has a wonderful statement about attitude. He says,

The longer I live the more I realize the impact of attitude on life. Attitude, to me, is more important than facts. It is more important than the past, than education, than money, than circumstances, than failures, than successes, than what other people think or say or do. It is more important than appearance, giftedness, or skill. It will make or break a company... a church... a home. The remarkable thing is we have a choice every day regarding the attitude we will embrace for that day. We cannot change our past... we cannot change the fact that people will act in a certain way. We cannot change the inevitable. The only thing that we can do is to play on the one string we have and that is our attitude... I am convinced that life is 10 percent what happens to me and 90 percent how I react to it. And so it is with you... we are in charge of our attitudes.

If Swindoll is right, 90 percent is a lot of control, and we can direct our day by choosing how we react to what happens to us. We do this by choosing our attitude. Every day, make sure you choose the best attitude you can and then work to maintain that attitude all day long. Do this every day, and life will go better.

❖❖❖❖

◆ Recall what your Voice of Conscience said to you this morning.
◆ Did you get off to a good start?
◆ If not, did you catch yourself in the process of choosing to have a bad day?
◆ Did you challenge your thinking?
◆ Remember to listen to the Voice of Conscience each morning, and if you don't like what you are hearing, change it.

Lesson 11

Automatic Thinking

A man's what he thinks about all day long.

~ Ralph Waldo Emerson

We create our own reality with our thinking. Something happens, and we think about it. What we think determines our reaction and experience. Our experience becomes our reality.

Our minds are always busy making meaning of life events. The problem is that we don't always know we are doing it. Over time, this making of meaning becomes automatic and happens outside of awareness. It is automatic because we have practiced it so often.

Automatic thinking is like the experience of learning to drive a stick-shift car. Did you learn to drive a standard transmission? Do you remember what it was like? You had to concentrate very hard on coordinating your hands and feet. With one hand on the steering wheel and one on the gearshift, you had to use your foot to press the clutch at just the right moment to change gears. If it was not done smoothly, you either choked down or did the "bunny hop" as you stopped and started, up and down the street. Improvement came with practice, and today you can drive across town, play a CD, talk on a cell phone, and arrive at your destination without really knowing how you did it. You no longer have to think about every move you make because it is automatic. Changing gears and steering occur without your awareness. You only pay close attention in an emergency.

Your thinking is the same. You have practiced certain thoughts and reactions so many times that they are automatic. You make a mistake and immediately think, "I can't do anything right." A co-worker is rude, and you say to yourself, "She's out to get me again." Someone cuts you off in traffic and you think, "What an idiot." These automatic responses produce a mood, influence your behavior, and create your reality. You never stop and challenge what you think because you are not aware of the process. What you tell yourself just seems to be the truth. You *do* always mess up, your coworker *is* out to get you, or the world *is* full of jerks.

Other possibilities exist. If you learn to pay attention to what you say to yourself, you can challenge it. You can make a different choice. Is it true that you *always* make a mistake? Could the boss have just criticized your co-worker and is that why she was upset? Was the other driver rushing to the hospital? If you see another possibility, you get another reality and a different experience. Automatic thinking can create trouble that you don't need. It can create a distressing reality that is based only upon your habitual thinking pattern.

Learn to pay more attention to what you say to yourself. Look for other explanations for what happened. Consider the possibility that your first thought may not be right. Challenge your thinking and give life the best meaning that you can.

❖❖❖❖

Here are some common automatic thoughts. Can you think of others that you use?

- ◆ "I am so stupid."
- ◆ "He is a real jerk."
- ◆ "I look terrible again."
- ◆ "Nothing ever goes my way.'
- ◆ "I never get what I want."
- ◆ "They must do what I want."
- ◆ "My luck will never change."

Lesson 12

Giving Up Perfection

We set up harsh and unkind rules against ourselves. No one is born without faults.

~ Horace

Have you ever made a mistake? Of course you have. Everyone does. The problem is not making mistakes, but what you tell yourself when you make one. What did you tell yourself the last time you made a mistake? Whatever you said depends upon your rule about mistakes.

We all have "Rules for Living" that we usually learned early in life and apply to our daily experiences. Because we live in an achievement and success-oriented culture, a popular rule is, "When you do anything, do it right." Our parents, teachers, coaches, and friends helped us learn this rule. If we adopted it as our own, it may have been translated as, "I should be thoroughly adequate and competent in everything I do." Accept this rule and you become a perfectionist. You won't like mistakes because mistakes are "bad" and something to be avoided.

If you are a perfectionist or just like to "do things right," then whenever you make a mistake, the Voice of Conscience—the "little voice" that talks to you—speaks up. The mistake may be big or small, but the Voice of Conscience always speaks up and says something like, "Look at that. What is wrong with you? Can't you do anything right? You will never learn. Why don't you just give up?" These thoughts may occur so quickly that you don't know you had them.

Soon, you are feeling down. Your sadness, anger, and frustration are increasing. If someone asks what is wrong, you point out the mistake, whatever it might be, and say, "Look at this mess. Anyone would be upset." You are claiming it is the mistake that has created your mood and behavior.

The reality is that you have created your mood and behavior with your inner dialogue of name-calling and criticism. The problem is that you are applying a bad rule about mistakes. It may have been a good rule and kept you out of trouble when you were six years old, but it is not a good rule now that you are an adult. It is time to change the rule. What would be a better rule?

In reality, what is a mistake? To find out, just recall how you learned to ride a bike. What is the first step in learning to ride? Falling off. You lean too far to the right and what happens? You fall. Next, you lean too far to the left and you fall again. Fall off and get back up enough times and you will learn to balance and ride the bike. *A mistake is always the first step in learning.* Success comes from mistakes. This is good news. This is wonderful news, in fact. With this new rule, the inner dialogue of the Voice of Conscience can change.

With your new rule, what should you say to yourself when you once again make a mistake? Something like, "Great! Wonderful! Now I can learn something." You will be energized and feel excited, challenged, and motivated. You will get busy and work harder.

Examine your rules about mistakes. What do you say when you confront failure? Is it positive or negative? Does your rule motivate and empower you or does it rob you of energy? Do you have a good rule? Do you like it? Just learn to listen to what you say to yourself. If you don't like what you hear—then change the rule. You are the rule maker. You can create a new rule for yourself. There are lots of rules about mistakes. Choose one you like and apply it.

❖❖❖❖

- ◆ Recall a recent mistake.
- ◆ Was your reaction one of excitement or dismay?
- ◆ What did you tell yourself about the mistake?
- ◆ Do you need to change your inner dialogue?
- ◆ List four positive statements about mistakes.

Lesson 13

Arguing with Yourself

*It was completely fruitless to quarrel with the world, whereas
the quarrel with oneself was occasionally fruitful and always,
she had to admit, interesting.*

~ May Sarton

Do you ever argue with yourself? Maybe something happens
that you don't like, so you start thinking about it. The Voice
of Conscience speaks up. Actually, it is sometimes more like two
voices. My young nephew tells me that it is like having an angel on
one shoulder and a devil on the other, and both are chattering away
at once. You are arguing with yourself about the pros and cons of
the situation. In this argument with yourself, do you usually win or
lose?

You will always win just by having the argument. Having the
argument means that you are trying to be objective about whatever
has happened. You are trying to look at both sides of an issue in
order to make the best decision you can and to choose the most
appropriate response. The real problem arises when you don't
argue with yourself because then you see only one point of view,
and it seems to be *the reality*. This one point of view is always
either black or white, and this is rarely true of life. With just one
point of view, you may foolishly rush in and create problems you
don't need.

Learn to argue with yourself, and see if you can make life go
better. Suppose that you are angry with a sales clerk who was short-
tempered with you. How did you get angry? You did it by thinking
about what happened. It is what you think her actions mean that
makes you angry. Your Devil Voice may be saying, "How rude and
inconsiderate. Who does she think she is? She can't get away with
this." While the Angel Voice may say, "Poor thing. She must be

having a bad day. I wonder what has happened to her. Maybe she has a headache." The Devil Voice butts in with, "That is no excuse. She should have stayed home. Call the manager and get her fired." The more compassionate Angel Voice is saying, "Now, that won't help anything. Just be nice. Tell her you are sorry that she is having a hard time." Back and forth and back and forth the argument goes, but by arguing with yourself, by thinking it through, you don't go into immediate action. You slow yourself down, so you can make a deliberate choice about your response.

You will always win the inner argument just because you had it. By arguing with yourself, you have challenged your assumptions and taken control of your behavior. Do this often enough, and you will realize that life does not make you respond in any manner. You always choose your reaction based upon your thinking or attitude about what is going on around you.

Remember, listen to your Devil Voice and listen to your Angel Voice, and then make the best decision you can. Learn to argue yourself into a reasonable judgment and life will improve.

❖❖❖❖

- ◆ Can you tell your Angel Voice from your Devil Voice?
- ◆ What does your Angel Voice usually tell you?
- ◆ What does the Devil Voice say?
- ◆ How do you referee between the two in order to decide what to do?

Lesson 14

How to Double Your Trouble

Who of you by worrying can add a single hour to his life?
~ Saint Matthew

Life always changes. It is not static. Nothing stays the same. Some changes we like, and others we don't. Some please us, and others scare us. A well-known scripture (Matthew 6:34 from the NIV translation) tells us, "Each day has enough trouble of its own." While this is true, most of us take whatever trouble we are given and immediately start making it worse than it is.

The process of making things worse than they are is called worry. When worrying you reach out into the future and imagine bad possibilities. You think, "Gee that would be terrible." And, "I don't think I could stand that." Or, "If that happens, I'm done for." You bring these possibilities into the present moment and convince yourself they are going to happen. They become your new reality. You have added to your trouble by making things worse than they are.

Here is the easiest way to double your trouble. It only takes three magic words and almost everyone knows them. Whenever anything happens that you don't like just use your magic words. Quickly turn to someone and say, "It's not fair." Immediately, you will have two problems. You have the reality of whatever has happened, plus the fact that you are angry or hurt because it is unfair. You may begin to complain bitterly about the unfairness, saying, "I shouldn't be treated this way." Or, "No one should have to put up with this. They can't get away with this. I'll show them." And so on.

Sometimes people become more upset about the perceived unfairness than the real problem. They can't seem to accept and deal with the event as it is. They spend all of their energy being angry rather than working on the problem. No progress is made because they distract themselves from the real issue.

The reality is that life *is* unfair. Unfortunate things happen to all people. Bad things do happen to good people. We must learn to accept the negative events of life; yet, we must not give up in despair or distract ourselves away from issues that can be resolved.

Sometimes, we can and should challenge the unfairness of life. Sometimes, it may be an issue of justice as in human rights violations. In these instances, if we try to make things right, we may be able to succeed. At other times, the unfairness will just be unfortunate and cannot be changed, as in the unfairness of an untimely loss that cannot be undone. This dilemma is captured in several verses from the well-known Serenity Prayer.

God, grant me the serenity to accept the things I cannot change, courage to change the things I can, and the wisdom to know the difference. ~Reinhold Niebuhr

This prayer says change it if you can. If you can't change it, accept it, but, most importantly, learn to tell the difference between what you can change and what you cannot change. We all need the wisdom to know the difference between these two things.

Always work on the problems you have, and don't get lost in issues of fairness. Work on them whether they are fair or not. If you work on a problem, you may fix it, even if it is not fair. Dwelling on anger and resentment about life's unfairness gets you nowhere. Don't spend time complaining. Accept the reality of the situation, whatever it is, and work for change.

❖❖❖❖

- Think of three things you have recently worried over.
- What was the worst outcome that you imagined?
- Did it happen? Did it come close to happening?
- Did you in fact worry for nothing?
- How can you learn to recognize unproductive worry?

Lesson 15

Changing Your Mind

Progress is impossible without change, and those who cannot change their minds cannot change anything.

~ George Bernard Shaw

How many of your problems could be solved by something as simple as changing your mind? All of the daily problems we face exist in our minds because in order to have a problem we must be thinking about it, and what we think may make the problem worse than it actually is.

For many of us it comes naturally to always imagine the worst and then to forget that we only imagined it. We take our imagination for the truth. While what we are worried about could happen, usually, it does not. We create unnecessary mental anguish through worry.

Suppose you are sick and visit your doctor to have some tests run. In the few days it takes to get the results, your busy mind can convince you that you must be seriously ill. You see yourself incapacitated, and even begin to plan your funeral, only to be given the good news that everything is normal. You created more misery than you needed.

If you can catch yourself in the midst of such exaggerated thinking and just change your mind by redirecting your thinking, life can get better. Changing your mind, however, is hard work because to do it you must think about *how* you think. You must pay attention to the inner chatter of the Voice of Conscience, and when you catch it exaggerating or talking nonsense, call a time-out and challenge the dialogue.

With regard to your doctor visit, when your mind wanders to the worst, stop and come back to the facts you have. Don't add to them. Remind yourself to practice patience and wait to hear from your physician.

If the workplace rumor is that layoffs are coming and you soon catch yourself standing in the unemployment line of your mind, stop! Bring yourself back to reality—nothing has happened yet. It is just a rumor. Turn off the negative fantasy machine, and life will get better.

Learn to change your mind by monitoring your thinking. When you catch your mind racing down the wrong path, put on the brakes, and turn around. You will create less misery. Practice thinking about how you think, and your problems may well decrease. Learn to catch your mind in action, and always make the more optimistic choice.

You can begin this process right now. Start thinking about how you think and just continue to do so all day long. When you find yourself thinking "nonsense" and adding to your trouble, just stop and come back to the current reality. Do this all day today. Now, continue to do it all day, every day for the rest of your life, and life will begin to improve.

Most people, upon hearing this advice, throw up their arms in despair and say, "It's too hard. Can't I just do it a few weeks and stop?" The answer is, "No!" That would be like successfully dieting two weeks and stopping. The weight soon returns.

The simple reality is that you have no choice about whether you will do it or not. Every day, you *will* think and create reality in your mind. You cannot avoid it. You are always thinking. The only choice you have is whether you will do it consciously or unconsciously. Will you do it and know that you are doing it, which means you are in control and can change it, or will you forget about your thinking, feel like a victim, and believe that others control your life?

Each day, choose to think about how you think. Each day, carefully listen to what you say to yourself, and choose your best attitude. Change your mind, and take control of your life.

❖❖❖❖

- Have you ever changed your mind and had a problem disappear?
- Have you ever received information that suddenly gave you a new perspective and a new point of view?
- The next time you are upset over a situation, don't focus so much on what happened. Instead, ask yourself, "What have I been thinking?"
- Can you change your thinking and solve a problem? Does changing your mind help?

Lesson 16

How to Change Yourself

... structures of which we are unaware hold us prisoner.

~ Peter Senge

Have you ever wanted to change something about yourself? You must first identify what to change. Find something about yourself that you don't like or that causes you problems. It might be that you are too critical of others. Maybe, you are too passive and can't say, "No." Maybe, you avoid exercise. Or, it might be that you work too much and won't slow down.

Once you identify what you want to change, just begin to observe yourself on any ordinary day. Observing yourself is the process of introspection. It is watching what you do and asking why you do it. Introspection is thinking about and catching yourself in action.

It can be risky. You may learn more than you wanted to know. You might learn things about yourself that are distressing. Once you gain such an insight into yourself, it is hard to give it up, and it will begin to change you. Thomas Mann said, "Introspection is the first step towards transformation...after knowing himself, nobody can continue being the same."

So, on any ordinary day, pick out a behavior to change, and then just watch yourself. Soon, that Voice that talks to you, the Voice of Conscience, will speak up and say something like, "Damn, you just did it again. You just criticized that person." Or, "You said 'Yes' when you should have said, 'No.'" Or, "You took the elevator when you could have climbed the stairs."

Whenever this Voice speaks up like this, it is good news. In fact, it is time to celebrate. You are making progress. Before, you always did the same thing, but you thought it was fine. You didn't even realize that it was a problem. Now, you have caught yourself after the fact. You are becoming more aware of what you do.

Just keep observing yourself and soon the Voice will say, "Here you go. You are doing it again." And, once again, you go ahead and do it. You have caught yourself in action again but not soon enough to stop. You are still operating on automatic, but you are making more progress.

With even more self-observation the Voice now says, "Look out! You are about to do it again." And once again, you do. You are catching yourself in action sooner and sooner. You are becoming more and more aware of what you are doing and building the momentum for change, but you can't stop yourself yet.

Eventually, the Voice says, "You are about to do it." But this time you don't do it. You make another choice. You have learned enough to catch yourself before you act. You no longer respond in an automatic manner, but can make a meaningful choice about what to do in a specific situation. You are more in control of yourself and can give up the problem behavior.

Once you understand yourself and your problem behavior, you grow and develop into a more mature person and do not fall back into the same old pattern. Each time you successfully change one of your problem behaviors, look for a new one, and just begin to observe yourself once again on any ordinary day. Soon, that Voice of Conscience will speak up and begin guiding you towards more change.

❖❖❖❖

- ◆ Begin the process of self-observation today.
- ◆ Choose a behavior to change.
- ◆ Try to catch yourself in the action of doing it once again.
- ◆ Become more aware of what you do, so you can take more control of your life.

Lesson 17

The Secret of Changing Others

Everybody thinks of changing humanity and nobody thinks of changing himself. ~ Leo Tolstoy

Have you ever tried to change someone? Have you ever tried to make another person be just a little bit different so that your life would be better? Maybe you wanted him/her to put the cap back on the toothpaste or to replace the toilet tissue so that it unrolled in the *right* direction. Perhaps it was a bigger problem, like getting someone to be more considerate, or to stop complaining all the time, or to give up a bad habit. Were you successful? Most likely, you were not. Changing others is very hard work. In fact, it may be impossible.

What is possible is to change yourself. If you change yourself, the surprise is that others may change as well. They change, not because you were trying to change them, but because they must change if you change. They cannot remain in the same relationship with you, if you are now different.

Suppose that others take advantage of your kindness? They always want to borrow something. They want you to run an errand and then baby-sit. Next, they want to borrow money. If you are reluctant and don't want to meet their requests, they beg, plead, or create such guilt that you give in and say, "Yes."

Later, you are angry and frustrated for having allowed yourself to be "used" once again. You ask these people to stop demanding so much and complain to them, "It just can't go on any longer." But each time they ask, you say, "Yes." Your effort at changing them is not working.

What if you changed instead? What if you began to say "No?" Often we are in the habit of saying "Yes" because we want to be liked. We don't want to upset anyone. We want life to go smoothly, but such effort hardly ever works. Eventually, it comes down to this question: "Do you want to be liked or respected?" Respect is usually the better choice. You can earn respect by simply saying, "No." Just say "No" and mean it.

The problem is that if you have habitually been saying "Yes," others may not believe it when you say "No." They certainly won't like it. So, they will ask again and again, putting pressure on you to say, "Yes." This is the critical moment. You must continue to say "No." If you say "Yes" just once, others will know that under pressure you will cave in. Stick to your answer of "No," and they will learn that you mean it.

Once others realize you have changed, they will also change. The change could be that they leave and do not come back, in which case you have not really lost anything, or they may stop asking for so much, and develop respect for you and your word.

So, it is possible to change others, but you do it by changing yourself. Focus your energy on what you want and desire and take a stand. Change yourself and see what happens.

❖❖❖❖

- Think of how you recently tried to change another person.
- Did you succeed?
- What could you change about yourself that might cause that person to change?
- Could you be more specific with that person about what you are willing and not willing to do?
- Could you ask for what you want?
- Will you challenge yourself to change first and see what happens?

Lesson 18

The Power of Four-letter Words

If you wish to know the mind of a man, listen to his words.
~ Chinese Proverb

How many four-letter words do you know? How often do you use them? Are they helpful? How about these four-letter words: life, love, fear, hate, hope, risk, and mind?

"Life" is a four-letter word full of possibility and potential. It has a possibility for joy but also a potential for misery. In life, your current experience colors your outlook. If life is not going well, many "expletive deleted" four-letter words can be used to describe it.

When life is good, however, a specific four-letter word is usually involved. This word is "love." With hearts full of love life goes better. When you are busy giving love, you have a positive influence on others. When you are receiving love, your spirits are lifted. Love brings you into communion with those around you and provides for an atmosphere of understanding and concern.

"Fear" is also a four-letter word. It often disrupts life. Fear can become a block to love. Out of fear, you hold back on your emotions, pull away from others, and isolate yourself. You may lash out in anger at those who frighten you only to get anger in return. Fear robs life of its positive potential. Fear can lead to "hate," a four-letter word that guarantees misery.

To overcome fear and avoid hate, you must have "hope," another four-letter word. You must be able to see through fear into a better possibility. You must use hope to become optimistic and to learn to express love with the expectation of a positive response. Hope offers the courage to take a chance—to take a risk. "Risk" is another of those four-letter words, but one that is enlivening.

Whether or not you take a risk depends upon your "mind," once again a four-letter word. Your mind provides your outlook on life. It is where your attitude resides, and it is the home of that small Voice of Conscience that talks to you. From your mind you look out upon life and choose a viewpoint of good or bad, positive or negative, or of hope or fear. This is an intentional choice. It is one for which you are responsible.

Your choice of viewpoint is critical to having a good life. When life is not looking good, re-evaluate your attitude, take a risk, and change your mind. Every day you have the opportunity of choosing a new viewpoint for life. Each morning the Voice of Conscience talks to you and sets the tone for your day. Listen carefully to what you say to yourself. What kind of four-letter words do you hear? Be sure you choose the best four letter-words you can and see if life goes better.

❖❖❖❖

- ◆ Listen for the four-letter words used around you.
- ◆ Are they positive or negative?
- ◆ How many positive four-letter words can you identify?
- ◆ Each day choose one positive four-letter word and use it as a focus for the day.

Lesson 19

Mind Over Matter

Why should we think upon things that are lovely? Because thinking determines life. It is a common habit to blame life upon the environment. Environment modifies life but does not govern life.
~ William James

In life a lot of things can matter to us. What matters to you? For example, the type of car you drive or the name brand of the clothes you wear. How much you weigh? Your age? What others think of you?

Have you said to someone, "It doesn't matter?" What did you mean? Has anyone ever asked you, "Does it matter?" What did they want to know? What are we talking about? What is it that matters? What does matter mean?

Something matters when it concerns us. Something matters when it is important. It matters when we take it seriously. If we don't take it seriously, it doesn't matter. What do you take seriously? What matters to you? What matters to you depends upon what you mind.

Have you ever been asked, "Do you mind?" It might be, "Do you mind if I smoke?" It means do you care. It means does it matter. Mind and matter are connected. If you mind, then it matters.

As a child you may have heard the refrain, "Sticks and stones may break my bones, but words can never hurt me." This is true. Words alone cannot hurt you. Words only hurt if they matter. Words only hurt if you mind. It is your response to the words that determines how you react.

Suppose that someone insults you by calling you "stupid." Does it matter? Well, it does if you mind. If you mind, you could start thinking, "Who do they think they are? Nobody can treat me this way. They won't get away with it. I'll show them." Now you are caught in a mood of anger because it matters. Or, you could think, "I guess they are right. I just can't do anything. Why do I bother to try?" Again, it matters because you mind, and you allow yourself to slip into a state of sadness and self-criticism.

A third possibility is that you don't mind because you don't take it seriously. You might think, "Well, that's their opinion, but I know it is not true. It is rude, but maybe they are having a bad day." You pay it no mind. It doesn't matter. You don't get angry or sad. You don't dwell on it all day or create misery for yourself.

Here is the secret of mind over matter. *If you don't mind, then it doesn't matter.* Be careful of the things you mind. Be careful of what matters. Intentionally make these choices. Decide what you will take seriously, and what you will overlook. Some things matter, and they need to matter. They are important. Other things don't matter. They are of small consequence. Learn to tell the difference. Learn to practice mind over matter and see if life goes better.

❖❖❖❖

◆ Has anyone recently hurt your feelings?
◆ Recall what they said or did.
◆ What did you tell yourself about it?
◆ Did you take it seriously? Did you make it matter?
◆ What were your options? Could you have chosen a different response?

Lesson 20

Catching People Being Good

If each of us were to confess his most secret desire, the one that inspires all his plans, all his actions, he would say: "I want to be praised."
                                                            ~ E.M. Cioran

Everyone has a job. It might be an official job where you get paid, or it could be an informal job where others have certain expectations of you. Perhaps you volunteered to coach the church softball team or promised that you would cut the grass at home this weekend. Your job performance is evaluated by what you do. It can be good or bad.

Sometimes you might want someone to do a better job. Maybe it is at work where you need the reports turned in on time. Or, you want friendlier customer service. It could be at home where you want Susie to keep a neater room and Johnny to take the garbage out on schedule. Perhaps you would like a shorter sermon from your minister or a sweeter disposition from your spouse.

The secret to getting better job performance, to getting what you want from others, is giving feedback. But not just any kind of feedback. You have to catch others being good and tell them. Catch them doing what you want and then let them know. Tell them how much you appreciate it. Reward them for good performance.

This is not what usually happens. At home or work, you often only hear when things are wrong. You only get negative feedback. You only hear criticism. When you do well, there is silence. For example, your boss may have told you that when you aren't hearing from him/her things are okay. The problem with this management strategy is that if you only hear feedback when it is bad, you begin to dread any feedback because it feels like punishment.

There is an old saying that "No news is good news." This is not true. No news is just *no* news. It is an absence of information. No feedback is just no information. A lack of feedback does not help anyone to do a better job. What does help is timely feedback that points out what is right. Being told you are doing it right creates enthusiasm and motivates you to do more. It also builds a positive relationship and is good for morale.

So, if you want life to go better, learn to catch people around you being good. Catch them doing it right and tell them. Learn to look for the positive and not the negative.

The next time the preacher has a short sermon, tell him how much you liked it. You may get more short sermons. When your spouse is being nice, express your appreciation. Find something neat in Susie's room and tell her how good it looks. Praise Johnny whenever the trash is taken out, even if it is not on schedule.

Learn to speak up when you catch people being good. Reward good job performance and see if life goes better.

❖❖❖❖

- How often do you give positive feedback?
- Who can you catch being good today?
- Did anyone catch you being good?
- How do you react to positive feedback?

Lesson 21

Self-Worth and Self-Esteem

A person's worth is contingent upon who he is, not upon what he does, or how much he has. The worth of a person, or a thing, or an idea, is in being, not in doing, not in having.
~ Alice Mary Hilton

How do you feel about yourself? Is it good or bad? How you feel about yourself is self-esteem. It is your perception of how you are doing in the world. Self-esteem goes up or down depending upon what is happening to you. Get an "A" on a test and you feel great but if you fail, you feel terrible. Self-esteem is changeable.

Self-worth differs from self-esteem. Self-worth is what you are born with. As one of the creations of the universe you are worthwhile and have value that cannot be taken from you. You can't lose it, but you can lose sight of it. You can forget your value. A universal spiritual teaching helps us to re-focus on our self-worth and hold on to it. "Love your neighbor as yourself" is the Christian version, but the teaching is found in all major religions.

When you love your neighbor as yourself, with whom do you begin? Who do you love and value first? Is it your neighbor or yourself? As a psychologist, I have found that many people misunderstand this teaching. They think it begins with the neighbor. They focus on the neighbor so exclusively that they neglect themselves. They give and give to others until they give out, and then they collapse into a depression. Once depressed, such people cannot help themselves or anyone else.

Many of us were taught to focus on the neighbor and not on ourselves. As children, we were told not to brag or be selfish. As teenagers we wanted to be accepted; so, we may have minimized our accomplishments to avoid appearing conceited. As adults we may have developed a false humility in order to avoid looking prideful. By underrating ourselves, we may have come to dislike ourselves and believe that we don't deserve anything good. Self-esteem suffers, and self-worth is forgotten.

The reality is that "loving your neighbor as yourself" begins with you. You must love and value yourself if you are to love others. You have to respect yourself and acknowledge your own self-worth. You must take care of yourself so that you can love and help your neighbor. Does this make you selfish? No. It makes you responsible.

Suppose that you are caring for a very sick person, perhaps a parent or a spouse, with a debilitating disease. Being determined that your loved one will never go to a nursing home, you work nonstop to meet all needs. Constantly available, you stay up to the wee hours of the morning, and then get up early. In addition to caring for your patient, you also have a job, as well as all the responsibility for managing the household. Over time, as your loved one's condition worsens, you redouble your efforts at providing care until your health begins to suffer. Eventually, your neglect of yourself causes a collapse into illness and forces you into bed. Now, with no one to provide care, your loved one must go to a nursing facility—the very thing that you did not want.

What should you have done? You should have been responsible enough to take care of yourself by keeping your energy up. How could you do it? Perhaps by asking family and friends for help, taking breaks, setting limits, or saying no to some requests. Maybe by going to a movie, taking a walk, or just sitting down long enough to relax.

Don't neglect others by neglecting yourself. First, love and value yourself and then you can love your neighbor. Don't forget your self-worth. Each day, make sure that you take good care of yourself so that you *will* be able to take care of your neighbor.

❖❖❖❖

◆ Recall a time when you felt really good about yourself.
◆ What was going on in your life at that time?
◆ How were you taking care of yourself?
◆ List several things you were doing then.
◆ Are you still doing these things now?
◆ Choose several simple ways to nurture yourself and practice them every day.

Part Two

Lessons for Coping:
Getting Through the Hard Times

Knowing the basic common sense information about how we create our reality and understanding the necessity for choice and action, provides a framework for improving our life experience. The challenges of daily life, however, will test our ability to use what we know. Remembering and practicing what we know is hard work. Often we think that we have resolved a problem only to have it reappear in some new form because we have slipped back into our familiar pattern. Recognizing our patterns before they become pitfalls is an important life skill.

Additionally, we have the demanding problem of coping with life in the Information Age. Simple daily tasks of living are increasingly more challenging because of the whirlwind of escalating change and stress. The normal ups and downs of life are becoming steeper and deeper. Stress takes its toll on all of us, and we need skills to manage it. Too much stress results not only in troubling physical symptoms but also brings the problems of emotional distress such as sadness, depression, frustration, and anger. We must learn how to cope with these potentially disabling emotions so that they do not drain away our resiliency. Being able to bounce back from adversity is a key skill in maintaining enthusiasm and keeping energy levels high.

The *Lessons* of Part Two discuss the need for an early recognition and response to life's potential pitfalls and offer strategies for "undoing" stress and building reserves of resiliency.

❖❖❖❖

Lesson 22

The Sidewalk of Life

Autobiography in Five Short Chapters
By Portia Nelson

Chapter 1
I walk down the street.
There is a deep hole in the sidewalk.
I fall in.
I am lost ....
I am helpless.
It isn't my fault.
It takes forever to find a way out.

Chapter 2
I walk down the same street.
There is a deep hole in the sidewalk.
I pretend I don't see it.
I fall in again.
I can't believe I am in this same place.
But, it isn't my fault. It still takes a long time to get out.

Chapter 3
I walk down the same street.
There is a deep hole in the sidewalk.
I see it is there. I still fall in ... it's a habit ... but, my eyes are open. I know where I am.
It is my fault.
I get out immediately.

Chapter 4
I walk down the same street.
There is a deep hole in the sidewalk.
I walk around it.

Chapter 5
I walk down another street.

Metaphors help us to understand life. A metaphor compares dissimilar things on the basis of some underlying theme, and a new insight or broadened understanding is created. Metaphors belong to the larger class of symbols. The English word "symbol" comes from two Greek root words meaning "to throw" and "together." Therefore, the word symbol means "to throw together," and this is what a symbol does. When you cannot say what something is, you can say what it is like. A symbol throws together a subject that is not understood with an image that is understood in an attempt to shed light on the subject. It compares one thing that we do understand with something that we do not understand in order to help us understand the thing that we do not understand. (Understand?) Symbols take us from a concrete, surface level of understanding to a greater depth of meaning. Metaphors do the same.

There are many metaphors for life. Everyone seems to know at least one because almost everybody has seen the movie *Forrest Gump*. In the movie, the main character, Forrest, tells us about life when he says, "Life is like a box of chocolates." Forrest not only provides the image, but he also tells us what it means. "You never know what you will get." Life can be seen as an adventure, full of surprises. Take a chance and see what happens. With a metaphor, however, there are many possible meanings. Others could be that "Life is sweet." Some chocolate is sweet, but not all. So, perhaps "Life is bitter." Or, maybe "bittersweet." Metaphors work on many levels.

The image of life as a journey is also a metaphor. Life's journey can be presented in a variety of ways. From our birth, life is taking us toward a goal with adventures along the way. Life may be seen as an ocean voyage across unknown depths where storms occasionally toss us around as we seek the safety of calm shores. An old bluegrass song tells us that life is like journeying on a mountain railway with hills, tunnels, dangerous curves, and the need for a brave engineer. Other metaphors speak of life as a wheel taking us through the circularity of change. Life may be seen as a spiral leading us upward in our growth toward maturity. Metaphors of life give us a vision of the life process and help us to understand what is required for the essential tasks of psychological and spiritual growth.

Portia Nelson's delightful and insightful story of the hole in the sidewalk provides another metaphor of life—life is a stroll down a somewhat hazardous sidewalk. Her story alerts us to the dangers of this stroll and identifies the key feature required to safely navigate life's sidewalk.

❖❖❖❖

- Think of songs you like. Are the titles metaphors for life such as "The Circle of Life" from the *Lion King* movie?
- What is your favorite metaphor for life?
- Has it helped you? If so, how?
- Can you think of a metaphor of which you don't approve? If so, why do you not like it? Is it too negative or too cheery?
- Can you create a new, positive metaphor for your life?

Lesson 23

The Sidewalk of Life: Falling In

Chapter One

I walk down the street.
There is a deep hole in the sidewalk.
I fall in.
I am lost .... I am helpless.
It isn't my fault.
It takes forever to find a way out.

Review chapter 1 above as you recall your journey down the Sidewalk of Life. What has your experience been? Have you had good times, for example, bright days full of sunshine with a breeze in the trees and spring flowers in bloom? Do you remember some of the difficult times, like a rainy, mud-splashed day when a dog chased you? Most importantly, in your journey, have you ever fallen into one of the holes in the sidewalk? Have you been minding you own business when unexpectedly the bottom fell out, and you suddenly found yourself in a pit of frustration, anger, anxiety, grief, or despair? Have you confronted loss, change, and challenge that caught you by surprise and seemed out of your control?

Chapter 1 is often true and states exactly how life is. Sometimes when walking down the sidewalk of life, you fall in a deep hole that is not of your own making.

- If you live on the coast during hurricane season, the winds and rains may come and damage your house.
- The company you work for may go bankrupt, and you lose your job.
- Returning to your car in the mall parking lot, you find that someone has smashed your fender.
- The death of a friend brings grief.

Any of these events can throw you in a hole of darkness, despair, anger, anxiety, worry, or grief. While it is true that you did not have anything to do with creating the situation, you must live with it. The hole can indeed be deep and dark, and you have to struggle long and hard to climb out of it.

Such is the nature of life. Some things are out of your control. Unexpected events happen. Change always occurs. The most that you can do is to adapt to change the best you can. You must struggle out of the holes into which you are thrown and journey on. Hopefully, you grow from such experiences and become a more mature person who is better able to cope with other pitfalls of life.

❖❖❖❖

♦ Recall some of the holes into which life has thrown you.
♦ What did you learn through the struggle to climb out?
♦ How were you strengthened?
♦ What scars, if any, do you carry?

Lesson 24

The Sidewalk of Life: Falling In, Again

Chapter Two

I walk down the same street.
There is a deep hole in the sidewalk.
I pretend I don't see it.
I fall in again.
I can't believe I am in this same place.
But, it isn't my fault.
It still takes a long time to get out.

With chapter 2 the question to consider is: Have you ever been in exactly the same hole more than once?

- Have you found yourself in the same bad relationship (but with a different person) for the twentieth time and wondered how all of these jerks and weirdos *find* you?
- Do you always get into the same type of conflict with every boss you have? They are so negative and critical, always expect so much, and make you feel miserable.
- Maybe you are caught up in the midst of the exact word-for-word argument with your spouse for the ten-thousandth time. He/she says *this* and you say *that* (just like you always do) and soon you fall into the same hole once again.
- Perhaps your son, mother, sister, or brother does that thing that they always do. It pushes your button; so, you respond as you always do, and the cycle of conflict begins once again.

Finding yourself in the same, familiar hole, you cannot believe that it has happened once more. You ask yourself, "Why does this always happen to me? Why do *they* always do this to me? When will they ever stop? Why can't they understand what they make me do?" You are convinced that if other people would just "act right," your life would go better. You begin working harder and harder to control others and to get them to change.

❖❖❖❖

◆ What familiar holes do you fall into again and again?
◆ Is there a pattern you can discover?
◆ Do you know what pushes your buttons?
◆ How can you disconnect these buttons so you do not always respond in the same way?

Lesson 25

The Sidewalk of Life: Taking Responsibility

Chapter Three

I walk down the same street.
There is a deep hole in the sidewalk.
I see it is there.
I still fall in ... it's a habit ... but, my eyes are open.
I know where I am.
It is my fault.
I get out immediately.

Chapter 3 challenges us to wake up. Fall into the same hole often enough and you may come to a realization. With the frequent occurrence of the same or similar events, you sense that such things do not happen by chance. Maybe such repetition signals a pattern that is not inflicted upon you by outside forces. Such a recurrence of events must mean that you are playing a role in creating them.

As we go along the sidewalk of life, we all fall into holes of psychological and spiritual distress. Sometimes it seems that we were shoved into the hole. Initially, it appears that it is not our fault to be in such a situation once again. As we continue in the journey of life, however, we often find ourselves falling into the same hole over and over. When we do, we are given the opportunity of recognizing that there is actually a pattern in our lives. Patterns do not exist until an event happens more than once. Only with repetition is it possible to see the pattern or cycle. Once the pattern is seen, we have the possibility of new insight.

The next time you find yourself once again in one of life's familiar holes, and are busy saying:

- "It is not my fault."
- "Don't blame me."
- "Who is responsible for this?"
- "They are doing it to me again."

Call for a time-out and look to see how you might be responsible for your situation. Ask yourself, "What did I do to get here? What role did I play in creating the circumstances that placed me in this hole?" The terrible truth is that if you are not responsible for being in this hole once again, you are in real trouble. Because if you are not responsible, it must mean that someone is. Maybe, it is not just one person but a group of people—like your coworkers or your family. Maybe everyone has decided to conspire against you.

If you are truly not responsible for your current situation, and you do not like being in this recurring hole, you face a dilemma. In order to get better, you first have to find out who is making you miserable. Next, you have to change that person, or that group of people to make them be exactly the way you want them to be so that you can be okay. Your life strategy becomes one of changing others. You have fallen into the trap of playing the game called, "Let's fix you."

Husbands, wives, parents and children often play this game. One spouse shows up at the counselor's office claiming that their mate is the problem. Parents bring in the child saying the child's behavior needs to change. Children say that their parents make them act this way. Employees blame the insensitive boss. The overworked boss criticizes the inefficient employees. No one is responsible for anything. Playing "Let's fix you" doesn't work.

Have you ever tried to fix someone? Of course you have. Maybe it was just changing a small child to become a little more the way you want him/her to be. Or, perhaps you have tried to make a few minor adjustments in another person's personality. It seems that if you just gave this person a little bit of a "tune up," you might be able to live together in peace. Did you succeed? The answer is "No!" Changing others is extremely difficult; in fact, it is virtually impossible. The other person may actually try to cooperate, but often cannot make or sustain the change. The problem is that your effort is directed in the wrong direction.

Fall into the same hole enough times, and you might awaken to the true nature of the problem. *You* are responsible for being there. *You* played some role in the process. *You* must change. Learning this is good news. If you can find out what you are doing and stop, you can avoid these holes into which you keep falling. Having some responsibility for your problems means that you have control. All you have to do is to change yourself, and the situation can improve. While this task is very hard, it is at least possible. Changing others is not.

- When you find yourself once again in that *same* bad relationship, but with a different person, you need to realize that it is *you* who is making the same mistake over and over. Maybe it is time to ask yourself, "What am I doing? How did I get here again?"
- When you are in that same tired, old argument, ask yourself, "What did I do create this situation?"
- When you are waking up with a hangover once again, ask what went wrong with your resolve to never drink again?

When you discover what you are doing or why you are doing it, change is possible. Now you can begin taking responsibility for yourself.

If you change yourself, your experience of the situation will change. Surprisingly, if you do this, the other people whom you wanted to change may change as well. You cannot change others by directly trying to influence them, but if *you* change, they may be forced to change as well. Once you are different and can maintain that difference, others around you are given the opportunity to change in relation to you. By effectively changing yourself, you may actually change another person, a group, and perhaps, the world, but you must start with yourself.

❖❖❖❖

- ◆ Identify one of your familiar holes in the sidewalk.
- ◆ How are you responsible when you fall into it again and again?
- ◆ Do you know what you do in order to get there?
- ◆ What other choices do you have?
- ◆ Can you exercise them?

Lesson 26

The Sidewalk of Life: Making Choices

Chapter Four

I walk down the same street.
There is a deep hole in the sidewalk.
I walk around it.

Chapter 4 is indeed a new chapter in your life. Once your responsibility is seen, you can start changing. You can begin avoiding the holes on your current street in life. You are now able to recognize what is coming toward you because you know your pattern. This knowledge gives you control and you can intentionally respond to life in a different manner. A different response offers new possibilities.

When a situation invites you into a familiar hole, you do not have to automatically enter. Suppose your friend, who has been awaiting your arrival to leave for a party, sarcastically says, "Well, you're late again, as usual!" Your typical response is to defensively reply, "Must you complain all the time?" Now, when you see that same "hole" of an argument and a bad evening coming, you make a different choice.

You realize that your friend has not only had the legitimate frustration of waiting but has also been worried about you. You could speak directly to these issues and say, "I am sorry I'm late. The traffic was terrible, and I couldn't get to a phone. I know that you were wondering what happened to me." Your choice allows your friend to acknowledge both concern and apprehension rather than just voice the frustration of waiting. The "hole" of another repetitive fight is avoided, and the evening has the potential of going well.

Developing insight into yourself, your habits, and your patterns of response helps you navigate around the predictable pitfalls of your life.

❖❖❖❖

- How do you recognize an approaching hole in the sidewalk?
- What are your early warning signals?
- Do you have any physical symptoms that warn you?
- How do you stay alert to looking for coming pitfalls?

Lesson 27

The Sidewalk of Life: A New Street

Chapter Five

I walk down another street.

Chapter 5 is a new day. Finally, you change streets. Your inner dialogue and behavior have changed so completely that the old pattern no longer occurs. Once on the new street, you must be careful because, unfortunately, this street will have its own holes. It will have holes that you have never seen before, but you now know the rules about the holes in the sidewalk. The first time that you encounter a hole, you should ask, "How am I responsible?" It may be that you are not responsible, but the sooner you ask this question, the sooner you can take charge of your life.

The sidewalks of life do not go in a straight line. They are also not flat. They are more like trails winding up a mountain until they reach the top. Each time you break out of an old pattern of thinking and living, you begin a new switchback that leads you ever upward toward the fundamental goal of life, which is wholeness. Fall into enough of the holes in the sidewalks and trails of life, and you may become whole.

To be whole is also to be healed. "Wholeness" and "healing" come from the same Old English root words as does "holy." Becoming whole means striving to be all that you can be, and this is ultimately a spiritual journey requiring the exploration of many possibilities. Working toward wholeness, you become more and more aware of what you do and why you do it. You learn that choices are made and that you are responsible for these choices. This spiral-like journey leads you upward toward psychological and spiritual wholeness. When seen from the proper perspective, the holes in the sidewalk that you encounter are actually life's invitations to grow.

❖❖❖❖

◆ Are you on a new street?
◆ Are you ready to grow?
◆ Are you open to the new "invitations" that will come?

Lesson 28

Change, Stress, and Information Overload

Change is the only evidence of life.

~ Evelyn Waugh

We change, whether we like it or not.

~ Ralph Waldo Emerson

Have you noticed how stressful life has become? Stress rushes at us from all directions. It comes from the big and small events of life, as well as the positive and negative ones. Sometimes life gets so stressful that people wish they could be stress-free, if only for a short while. This desire is unfortunate because we have a word to describe people who are totally stress-free. The word is *dead*. Most people do not want to be *this* relaxed.

Life is inherently stressful. We are always confronting potential stressors—those events that cause stress. As long as you are alive, you will encounter stress. Stress cannot be avoided because it comes from change, and change is everywhere. Change itself, however, is not the problem. Change has always been with us, and without it life would be pretty boring.

Heraclitus, the Greek philosopher, studied change and shed some interesting light on it. He described change as a flowing river and noted, "You cannot step into the same river twice." He also taught us that: "The only thing that is constant is change." With this teaching, Heraclitus was *both* right and wrong.

Change is constant in that it is always with us, but it has not stayed constant. Change itself has changed, becoming more rapid. In recent decades change has gained such momentum that it is unlikely to ever slow down again. As the speed of change increases, so does the level of stress. We are now confronting a greater rate of change than we have ever before experienced, and at the same time, we are required to make adaptations with ever-increasing frequency.

When a change begins, it may appear small, but soon it is much like an avalanche cascading downhill, gathering momentum and burying things in a flood of unexpected, ever-expanding consequences. In spite of the current rapidity of change, however, we will soon be looking back upon these times as "the good old days" when change was relatively slow, and stress was easy to manage.

Just how has change increased? The *change* of change is most evident when we look at the accelerated rate of growth in mankind's knowledge base. Assume that all the philosophical and scientific knowledge accumulated over the 50,000 years leading up until the year 1 A.D. equals one Unit of Information. The question to consider is: At what speed does knowledge grow?

How long did it take one basic Unit of Information to double? A study by French economist Georges Anderla found the answer to be 1,500 years, or until the sixteenth century. The next doubling of information, from two to four Units took only 250 years or up until 1750. By 1900, only one hundred and fifty years later, information had doubled again up to eight Units. The speed of doubling was getting faster and faster. Sixteen Units of Information was reached in 1950 with the passage of only fifty years, and this doubled again in just ten years to a total of 32 Units. Another seven years and it was at 64 Units, and then in just six years, the total had reached 128 Units of Information. This was in 1973, the year of Anderla's study. The doubling speed of information has continued to accelerate and is now estimated to occur about every 18 months. With the coming of the Internet, information in certain specialized areas may double every year.

No wonder you have a hard time keeping up with the latest data! Trying to stay current with the knowledge base of just a limited area of interest is nearly impossible. Move out of this familiar area and sifting through the maze of information is mind boggling.

We are seeing more and more specialization as people struggle to control the stress that comes from "keeping up" by limiting the size of the information pool with which they must be familiar.

Nevertheless, information continues to whirl all around us with an ever-increasing velocity.

Adding to the complexity of the situation, consider the distinctions that can be made between information and knowledge. In his bestseller, *Megatrends*, futurist John Naismith points out, "We are drowning in information but starved for knowledge." All of our rapidly doubling information may not have much utility because it might only consist of isolated bits of data such as discrete observations, single measurements, and unrelated facts. To be useful, this information must be organized. "Knowledge is information with structure," is the declaration of software entrepreneur Neil Larson. In the midst of a whirlwind of information, our challenge is to structure it into useful knowledge. Once organized as knowledge, it may be more manageable and, over time, as we add real life experience to our knowledge, we may transform it into the wisdom desperately needed to survive in the escalating Information Age.

❖❖❖❖

◆ How has the information glut affected you?
◆ How many magazines, newspapers, and journals do you read each week?
◆ What do you struggle to keep up with?
◆ How quickly does your knowledge base change? Is it stable or in flux?

Lesson 29

Computers and Stress

There are three roads to ruin; women, gambling and technicians.
The most pleasant is with women, the quickest is with
gambling, but the surest is with technicians.

~ Georges Pompidou

Technology is dominated by two types of people: those who
understand what they do not manage, and those who manage
what they do not understand.

~ source unknown

The computers helping us to manage the current deluge of information are the same computers that helped to create the flood. Computer technology also demonstrates a rapid acceleration of change. Moore's Law is the most cogent statement of this process. In 1966, Gordon Moore, the founder of Intel, stated that the power and complexity of the silicon chip would double every 12 to 18 months. This 18-month prediction has proven true. Today's computer chip is several million times as powerful as its predecessor of 30 years ago, and these powerful processors have ushered us into the Information Age.

Computer technology, the information highway, and the Internet, have created a new category of stress—techno-stress—the stress that comes from continually adapting to new technologies. First, you adapt to the electronic way of doing things, and then just when you finally master a challenging computer program, an upgrade occurs, and you must begin learning again. Or, another new and more challenging information system is integrated with yours, and you struggle to make them compatible.

Computer technology also creates a "data smog" of information that now whirls around us. It has been reported that managers in mid-level companies not only have to read a million words a week to stay current, but receive an average of 177 voice, fax, and e-mail messages per day. Spending just one minute per message takes up three hours of the day with trying to stay in touch. Managing your messages is no longer a sideline task, but it becomes your primary job.

People with high-level "busy-ness" are beginning to experience the latest diagnosis of "information fatigue syndrome." Information is wearing us out. In modern life we are receiving information at 400 times the rate of a Renaissance person. One weekday issue of the New York Times contains all the information that a person in the seventeenth century assimilated in their entire lifetime. Yet, today we try to browse through it in an afternoon while also watching television, carrying on a telephone conservation, and periodically checking our e-mail. No wonder we feel overwhelmed.

The rapid pace of modern life can be disturbing. "Time sickness," a new concept stemming from the effort to juggle too many options with too little time, is becoming prevalent. As we experience events happening faster and faster, we begin to expect everything to happen quickly. It becomes difficult to slow down. We actually become impatient with slower computers, which are still amazingly fast, when we have to wait an extra few extra seconds for something to happen. Frustration and stress arrive as we wait for the monitor screen to change.

Future shock, which is described as too much change in too short a time, has arrived. Symptoms of future shock appear as increased signs of dysfunctional behavior—irritation, frustration, confusion, and irrational acts. Look around you, at home and at work, or maybe in the mirror. What do you see? Maybe you and those around you are overly stressed by change and information overload.

We have moved out of the Industrial Age and into the Information Age where we are continually adjusting to new and changing situations. Over one hundred channels on cable TV bombard us with more information than we can assimilate. On the evening news, you learn in thirty minutes all of the major events of the day from around the world. As a member of the "global village," you now learn almost instantaneously, what in the past, would have taken months or years to know. The result is that you are more immediately impacted by a wide variety of world events, most of which is a plethora of bad news: crime, violence, disease, epidemics, natural disasters, and political conflict. Downsizing, restructuring, and re-engineering threaten formerly secure jobs, and family life is thrown into turmoil.

While a safe haven from change is sometimes temporarily found on a vacation or in a quiet stolen moment admiring the beauty of a flower garden from your office window, such moments of peace and serenity are often missing from modern life. It is hard to predict what will happen next. The rules are always changing, and the game is not the same.

❖❖❖❖

- How have you been affected by information technology?
- How many electronic gadgets do you use in a day?
- How do you cope with the impact of technology on your life?

Here are some ways to set limits on the information whirlwind.

- Turn off the pager when not at work.
- Don't answer every phone call.
- Don't take the cell phone to the beach or on vacation.
- Limit television watching.
- Get rid of the answering machine.
- Filter e-mail.
- Take a news holiday.
- Stop the newspaper.
- Don't take the laptop everywhere you go.
- Limit Internet surfing.
- Go on a "data diet."
- Meditate. Sit silently. Do nothing.

Lesson 30

Are You Stressed and Don't Know It?

For fast-acting relief try slowing down.

~ Lily Tomlin

In the midst of the incessant demands of modern life, people are often stressed and don't know it. People have become so accustomed to the symptoms of stress that they accept them as a part of daily life. Such symptoms of stress are thought to be normal, and it is believed that everyone has them.

Life *is* naturally stressful. It has always been so, but because we live in a time of rapidly increasing change, life is getting more and more stressful. Of the many daily changes you face, some will be perceived as threatening. Something changes, and you don't like it. Whenever threatened by anything, your body has only one response. Instantly, it goes into a stress reaction. In the whirlwind of change, it is possible to be in a mild stress reaction and not know it because you have gotten used to it. Stay in a state of emergency preparedness long enough and you begin to think that this state is normal. You no longer notice it. You habituate to the problem of stress.

Habituation means to become accustomed to something through prolonged exposure. It is like cooking fish for dinner one evening and noticing the "fishy smell" in kitchen as you do so. Soon the odor seems to disappear as you get used to it. The odor is still there, but you no longer notice it. If you take a walk in the fresh air after dinner, when you return you will once again become aware of the odor, and the habituation process starts over.

When stressful events in life are continually present, we get used to them and then no longer notice the stress reaction that is created. If the stress level in our life goes up, the stress reaction may increase and once again get our attention, but we soon habituate to this new level. Over time the stressful level of physiological arousal gradually intensifies, but we adapt and eventually think, "This, too, is normal." We become more and more stressed but do not realize it. Our bodies, however, are very much aware of this turbulent state of affairs.

Live in habituation to stress long enough and your body will eventually call your attention to it. You will notice a variety of physical symptoms as your body tries to tell you that something is wrong. Your physical symptoms are the natural result of living with a chronic, low-grade stress reaction. They signal that your stress level is too high and must be lowered. If you have adapted to the stress reaction, you may have forgotten what stress feels like and need to recall the signs and symptoms.

Recognizing Stress

Recognizing the stress response is easy. Just imagine that you are driving a car when someone suddenly pulls out in front of you. In this dangerous situation your body immediately responds with a stress reaction. What do you notice?

As your body goes into a stance of preparation getting ready to take action, all of your muscles tense up to help you respond to the danger. Your reflexes will be faster, and you can more quickly act with increased muscle tension. Tense muscles, however, need more oxygen, so your heart rate goes up. When your heart rate goes up, your blood pressure also rises. You breathe faster to get more oxygen into the blood stream. The belly tightens up as digestion comes to a screeching halt. This is not a good time to be leisurely digesting food, so the blood supply is diverted away from the belly to the large muscles that now need it. Along with these physical changes, you feel either anger or fear. All of these responses are your body's way of preparing you to run away if you can, or to fight if you must. This is the well-known "fight or flight" response.

If, while hiking in the woods, you suddenly encounter a rattlesnake on the trail, the stress reaction makes a lot of sense. Your body will instantly respond as it prepares you to either fight or run away. Flight is usually the best choice, but if the snake is at your feet when you first see it, you may have to defend yourself with your hiking stick.

When a car pulls out in front of you, you may have a fleeting fantasy that if you were driving an armored vehicle, like a tank, you would just keep driving and bump the other car off into the ditch. You may feel like fighting, but avoidance is the thing to do. Put on the brakes and turn the wheel.

When you avoid the accident, your body soon settles back down to normal. Muscles relax, heart rate comes down, blood pressure decreases, and breathing slows. Once you take action either through fight or flight and get out of the threatening situation, life returns to normal. This is how stress is always supposed to work in your life.

The problem with the stress reaction, however, is that it is built into our bodies through evolutionary history so we can protect ourselves from things that might kill us—things like saber-toothed tigers. We don't often confront such threats anymore. In modern life most stress does not come from things that threaten to physically harm us. It does not come from situations that you can actually fight or from which you can run away.

Most modern stress comes from psycho-social-emotional events. What does this mean? Well, there is a shorthand phrase for psycho-social-emotional events. It is "other people." In modern life other people cause you stress because modern stress comes from relationships you are in. It is important to remember, however, that as other people cause you stress, you do the same for them. Modern stress is a two-way street. It comes from family, friends, work, and church relationships. People say or do things that cause you stress. There might be job pressure, marriage problems, and financial difficulties. Johnny has school problems. Mom is in a nursing home.

These things you can't fight or run away from. If you try, the stress only gets worse.

Suppose you have a job. One day your supervisor stops you in the hallway and tells you that the report you just completed has several errors and must be corrected immediately before the staff meeting. Could this be stressful? If it is, you will notice your body's response. As your supervisor turns to walk away, your heart rate goes up, and your muscles tighten. Your breathing is fast, and your blood pressure rises. At this point, your body and its physical symptoms are sending you an important message. What is it?

You body is saying that a backhand to the face would probably solve this problem. A fight response is required. Or, maybe you should just start screaming and running. Run down the hallway, out the door, all the way home, and never come back. Maybe flight will help. Your body's only two options are fight or flight.

Hopefully, you realize that neither of these choices are good for your job security. Either one would only make matters worse and create more stress. So, if you can't fight or run, what do you get to do? Well, you get to "stew." You stew in the physiological juices of increased muscle tension, elevated heart rate, rapid breathing, raised blood pressure, and a knotted up stomach. You just *live* with it.

How you think will also influence your level of "stewing." As you recall your boss's comments, or as you tell your co-workers how you were mistreated, you relive the situation in your mind and add to your stress reaction. You may even remember a few things that happened last week and use them to add fuel to the fire. Stew long enough and over time you will start to notice physical symptoms such as headaches, backaches, chest pain, dizzy spells, or stomach problems. This is your body's way of saying—too much stress. Live with stress long enough, and you can get physically sick.

The first step in managing stress is to learn to recognize when you have it. Know the signs and symptoms of a stress reaction.

Look for them in your life. When you find them too frequently, you must take a deep breath and relax. Relaxation is the cure for stress.

❖❖❖❖

◆ What are your signs of stress?
◆ Read the list below and evaluate yourself. See if you can learn to recognize your stress signals.

Physical Symptoms	Emotional Symptoms
Headaches	Crying
Indigestion	Nervousness
Stomach aches	Boredom
Sweaty palms	Edginess
Sleep difficulties	Feeling powerless
Dizziness	Anger
Back pain	Loneliness
Racing heart	Unhappy for no reason
Restlessness	Easily upset
Tiredness	Irritation
Ringing in ears	Discouragement
Tense neck and shoulders	Overwhelming pressure

Behavioral Symptoms	Cognitive Symptoms
Excessive smoking	Unclear thinking
Bossiness	Memory loss
Overly critical of others	Lack of creativity
Grinding teeth in sleep	Constant worry
Overuse of alcohol	Loss of humor
Compulsive overeating	Poor concentration
Inability to get things done	Difficulty making decisions

Lesson 31

Positive Stress

Life is a Challenge—Meet It!
Life is a Song—Sing It!
Life is a Dream—Realize It!
Life is a Game—Play It!
Life is Love—Enjoy It!

~ Bhagawan Sri Sathya Sai Baba

In the current information revolution, change happens almost instantaneously. With all of this change rushing around us, life has become so stressful that people have actually been known to complain about it. Perhaps even you have uttered a few complaints.

The curious thing is that most people who complain about stress find at times that they don't have enough; so, they go out and look for more. Maybe you have done this. What were you doing the last time you went looking for stress on purpose?

You say you never intentionally look for stress? Well, consider this. Have you ever gone to an amusement park on purpose planning to ride the roller coaster? Have you tried white water rafting? Do you like scary movies? Ever been bored and wanted life to be more exciting? If so, then there is a good chance that you went looking for stress.

If we were to find you yelling and screaming on that roller coaster and called a "time out" to measure what your body was doing, we would find all of the physical signs of a stress reaction. We would find tense muscles, an elevated heart rate, raised blood pressure, rapid breathing, and a tight stomach. However, if we asked you what you were doing, you would say, "Having fun. It's challenging and exciting."

On the other hand, suppose that someone persuaded you to reluctantly board the roller coaster. Once it rolls away and cannot go back, you realize that this is a bad mistake. Now you are yelling and shouting and have all the physical symptoms of stress. If we asked what you are doing, what would the answer be? Most likely, that it is horrible and terrible, and that you will never do it again.

So, two people can be doing the same thing. One is having fun, and the other is not. One is stressed, and the other is not. What is the difference? It comes down to attitude and choice. If you feel in control of a situation because you choose to do it and if you think of it as exciting and challenging, it will be so. If you feel out of control or forced in to the situation and think of it as frightening, it will be scary and stressful.

In life there are two kinds of stress. We have positive stress that we like. It has a special name. It is "eustress." Eustress is stress that turns you on and makes life fun. We seek it out and will even pay money and travel long distances to get it—like that ski vacation you are planning or the adventure trip you want to take.

The other stress is "distress" or negative stress. This is the stress that wears you out. It usually shows up every day. It comes from both minor events and major hassles. You don't have to look for it. It finds you, and it is free. Over time too much distress, negative stress, can make you miserable and can even make you sick.

Watch out for negative stress. Learn to recognize it. Balance it with positive stress. Be sure you do something exciting every day. Challenge yourself to have fun on purpose. Learn to enjoy yourself, and life will go better.

❖❖❖❖

- ◆ Where do you get your positive stress?
- ◆ What challenges do you enjoy?
- ◆ What is your next adventure?
- ◆ What will you do to enliven life today?

Lesson 32

Controlling Stress

You cannot prevent the birds of sorrow from flying over your head, but you can prevent them from building nests in your hair.

~ Chinese Proverb

Every day is stressful. Sometimes the source of your stress is vague and hard to identify. At other times, you know exactly what is causing your stress. You can name it and point your finger at it. *It is this problem, this situation, or this conflict.* If you can name your stress, this is good news because you may be able to control it by taking action. If you know what is causing your stress, it may be possible to reduce, control, or eliminate it.

Suppose that you live in an apartment building with noisy neighbors upstairs and downstairs and are stressed out because you cannot sleep. You could solve this problem. You might move to a nice, quiet cottage in the country, and life would be good. You sleep all night, and your stress is gone. Before moving, however, you could complain to the neighbors, complain to the landlord, or call the police. By taking action you may reduce, control or eliminate your stress.

The problem with this strategy is that even when we can name our major stresses, we often feel ambivalent about them. We feel two ways at once.

What if you have a job that is slowly driving you crazy? On a really bad day, you decide to quit, but on the way to the front office you remember something pretty important about this job. It pays the bills. In fact, it pays them quite well. So, you turn around. You decide that you can do this job just a little longer. A few days later you get stressed again and decide to quit, but on the way to quitting you again remember the money and decide to stay. You go back and forth until eventually you decide not to decide, which, of course, is a decision, and you stay stuck in a bad situation. You are ambivalent and won't take action.

If it is not a job, it might be that on-again, off-again relationship in which you are involved. When the relationship is bad, you decide to get out, but the other person now straightens up and acts right so you decide to stay. Again, you go back and forth until you decide not to decide. Ambivalence leads to inaction, and you feel trapped. You choose to stay stuck in a stressful situation of your own making.

Remember, if you know what is causing your stress, taking action may help. The action you take does not require that you abandon the situation, but only that you do *something*. Politely asking your noisy neighbors to be quiet might be all that is needed. On your job you might only need a new schedule or a transfer to a less stressful department. Talking to your partner and going to counseling may help work things out. Just do something and life may get less stressful.

Don't decide not to decide. Don't choose to be stuck. Don't get mired in ambivalence. Remember that if you can name your stress, you may be able to reduce, control, or eliminate it. Always look for this option, and exercise it whenever you can.

❖❖❖❖

- ◆ Can you name three stressful situations in your life?
- ◆ What options exist to reduce, control, or eliminate them?
- ◆ Do you have any ambivalence about these options?
- ◆ What is the nature of your ambivalence?
- ◆ What action are you willing to take today?

Lesson 33

Stress and Your Health

I find, by experience, that the mind and the body are more than married, for they are most intimately united; and when one suffers, the other sympathizes.

~ Lord Chesterfield

Does your day begin with stress? Do you have a mad dash to get the kids to school and yourself to work? Does stress only increase from that point?

The first stress you encounter during the day gets the muscles tense, the heart racing, and the blood pressure up. Your breathing pattern increases while your stomach tightens. Irritation and frustration appear. With the stress cycle going strong, these symptoms just build up until after a day of stress, you begin to feel the effects. Aches and pains appear. Your energy drops. It becomes hard to concentrate even on simple tasks. You feel bad and just need to go to bed.

If such a pattern of stress goes on day after day and week after week, you are headed for problems. If you continue living with and adapting to chronic stress, your body will eventually attempt to get your attention and tell you that something is wrong.

While you may ignore early stress symptoms, the body does not. The body's message of too much stress is delivered through a variety of physical complaints like: headaches, neckaches, and backaches as well as other muscle and joint pain. Chest tightness, heart palpitations, shortness of breath, or dizzy spells occur. Problems with the stomach such as pain, cramping, spasms, or diarrhea may also appear. Emotionally you become generally keyed up and on edge.

While you may initially ignore such symptoms, ultimately they get your attention, and you decide you must be sick. If you are sick, you go to your doctor who listens to all your problems, orders tests, and helps you spend a lot of money. In about two weeks, you are called back into the physician's office and told something guaranteed to make you mad. "Good news," the doctor says. "There is nothing wrong." And you just sit there—with your headache, backache, or stomach ache, wondering, "How can that be? Why am I hurting so bad?"

Well, the "good news" is good news. What was the doctor trying to find? Evidence of disease. It can't be found. This is wonderful news. It means that you haven't hurt yourself—yet. However, if you keep living the same high-stress lifestyle for a few more months and return to the doctor, you may get the "bad news." You will have hurt yourself.

Your blood pressure which used to go up and down is now up and won't come down on its own. You need medication to control it. All that pain in your stomach is now an ulcer. Live with stress long enough, and it will make you physically ill. Furthermore, if you already have an illness, like diabetes or arthritis, then stress aggravates it, making it harder to control. Too much stress can be a dangerous problem.

Learn to recognize the symptoms of stress. Look for them in your life. Don't let stress build up until it reaches a dangerous level. Take breaks, slow down, and learn to relax. Don't let stress control you. Learn to control it.

❖❖❖❖

- Has your doctor ever given you the "good news?"
- Did you have too much stress?
- What changes did you make to control stress?
- Did these changes help?
- To avoid the "bad news," put some stress management skills into action.

Lesson 34

Learning to Relax

The time to relax is when you don't have time for it.
~ Sidney J. Harris

Some stress is good for you. It makes life exciting. Too much stress is bad for you and can wear you out. Too much stress creates both physical and emotional problems which can affect your daily life at home and work. Too much stress leads to irritation and frustration as well as poor concentration, attention and memory. It makes it hard to get through the day. When you are stressed out you make mistakes, and any job you are doing gets more difficult. Efficiency and productivity go down as you stop to correct the errors you made or to soothe the feathers you may have ruffled.

The fundamental problem with stress is that you can not make it go away. It is part of life. You cannot be stress free; so, the challenge is to learn to how to undo what stress does to you.

You might remember that the symptoms of a stress reaction are tense muscles, an elevated heart rate, heightened blood pressure, rapid breathing, and a tight stomach, as well as the energizing emotions of anger or fear. The stress reaction is your body's way of preparing you for fight or flight. Your body is trying to help you confront stress by either resisting it or by running away from it. In modern life, however, this strategy does not work. You can't fight or run away from most modern stress. It is just a part of daily life.

You can, nevertheless, cope with stress and to do this you must learn to relax—a special kind of relaxation in which you quickly and intentionally relax all the muscles of your body. Once the muscles relax, they need less oxygen and your heart rate is allowed to slow down. As a result, your blood pressure also comes down. As your muscles relax, your breathing slows to a deep, regular pattern, and your stomach calms. You begin feeling peaceful and refreshed and have more energy to face the rest of the day. Try relaxing like this twice a day, and you will be undoing what the stress reaction does to you.

How do you undo stress? First, set aside 10 minutes. Sit in a chair. Starting with your hands, tighten them into fists. Hold the tension 10 seconds. Now, relax the hands. Feel the difference. Notice how the muscles are relaxing. Do the same thing with the biceps. Raise both arms and create tension. Hold it 10 seconds and relax. Work your way up to your face and forehead, and then down to your chest and stomach, and finally to your legs, feet, and toes. Create and hold tension in all the major muscle groups. When you finish, you will be relaxed. You will have forced all the muscles into relaxation and will have undone what stress was doing to you. Practice this simple exercise every day and life will begin to go better.

❖❖❖❖

Here are the complete relaxation instructions.

Find a quiet place where you will not be disturbed for about 10 minutes. Dim the lights. Locate a comfortable chair in which you can sit up straight with your feet on the floor. Get comfortable. Pay close attention to how you feel. Notice any stiffness or tightness. Are there any aches or pains? Do you feel tense, frustrated, or keyed up? Later you can compare back and see if you have relaxed.

The systematic muscle relaxation procedure is as follows. Each time hold the tension for 10 seconds.

Take a deep breath, slowly let it out, and close your eyes. While sitting quietly and comfortably, bend your right hand back at the wrist and hold the tension. Hold it for 10 seconds. Now relax.

Next, do the same thing with the left hand. Hold the tension and now relax.

This time tighten both hands into fists and hold the tension. Feel it spread up the arms towards the elbows. Now relax.

Now bend both arms at the elbows and raise your hands up toward your shoulders. Tighten up the muscles in the biceps. Hold it. Now relax.

These three exercises have used the major muscles in the arms and have started them relaxing. If you don't move them around, they will continue to relax. As they become more and more relaxed, you can just forget about them.

Next, turn your attention to your face. For your forehead, raise your eyebrows up as far as you can and hold the tension. Now, all at once, relax them.

For your eyes, tightly squeeze the eyelids together. Hold the tension, let it build up, and now relax.

For your jaw, bite down and clamp your teeth together. Feel the tension along the jaw. Now relax.

These three exercises have started the face relaxing.

For your neck, just bend your head forward as if trying to touch your chin to your chest. Feel the tension along the back of the neck. Now relax.

For your shoulders, just raise them up as high as you can and notice the tension. Hold it. Now let them drop all at once and relax.

For your chest, you take a deep breath and hold it while

at the same time trying to touch your shoulder blades together by pulling your arms back. Hold it. Now relax.

For your stomach, you just pull in as if trying to touch your backbone. Hold the tension. Now relax.

For your back, you arch out and away from the chair and can feel tension along the spine. Now relax.

With your feet flat on the floor, press down and feel the tension spread up the back of the legs. Hold it. Now relax.

For the right thigh, raise your leg up in front of you and feel the tension build. Now relax.

Now do the same thing with the left leg and relax.

Finally, for your feet, bend your toes up as if pointing towards the ceiling, and feel the tension around the feet and ankles. Now relax.

Continue to relax for a few minutes and then slowly count to 10, take a deep breath, and open your eyes. Compare to how you were feeling before you started.

Practice this exercise twice a day.

◆   You can use these instructions by reviewing them to refresh your memory and then just do what they say. You could ask someone to slowly read them to you, or you could read them into a tape recorder and play them back for yourself.

◆   The relaxation exercise is also available from the Awakenings Web Site at www.lessons4living.com/ and can be listened to on-line.

Lesson 35

Using Your Imagination

When the imagination and will power are in conflict, are antagonistic, it is always the imagination which wins, without any exception.

~ Emile Coué

Our imagination can please us, scare us, or relax us. It all depends on what it is focused upon. Frequently, we use worry to frighten ourselves. Something happens that we don't like, and we begin imagining how bad it could become. We take an imagined future of bad possibilities and make it our new reality. We upset ourselves over what has not yet happened. We stress ourselves more than is needed.

The problem confronted when thinking about what might happen is that your body cannot tell the difference between what is real and what is just make-believe. When you are creating a fearsome fantasy of things to come, your body has no way of slipping around your mind to get outside and see what is really going on. This situation of worry is similar to waking up in the middle of the night from a nightmare with a racing heart, sweaty palms, and a sense of fear. This is actually a silly thing for your body to be doing because, after all, where is your body? It is safe in bed. Your body, however, is responding to the mental content of the dream. When you create a scary daydream of a negative future the same thing happens. Your body reacts to the imagined reality that you create by responding with a stress reaction.

You can reverse this process by using pleasant imagery to bring about a state of relaxation. As you practice the progressive muscle relaxation exercise you learned earlier, you can deepen the state of relaxation by adding a positive fantasy at the end. Just imagine that you are in one of your favorite peaceful, pleasant places. This might be the beach, mountains, a vacation spot, or a special place from your childhood. It could be someplace you have never been, like Hawaii. It does not matter what it is as long as it is peaceful, and you can immerse yourself in the image. While you are busy thinking about your pleasant place, you will not be distracting yourself away from your state of relaxation by worrying about a problem. Your imagination will help you to more deeply relax.

Create several images of pleasant places for yourself and practice using them to learn which ones work best for you. Using the imagery of a pleasant place while you are already relaxed will enhance the power of that image to induce deeper levels of relaxation through a process of conditioned learning. You will be teaching yourself to associate this image with increasingly deeper states of relaxation. Soon you will be able to use your pleasant imagery by itself to quickly undo stress. An additional advantage of using an image to relax is that you can use it anywhere.

Keep a list of your relaxing images available and use them as needed. Make life go better by using your imagination to manage your stress.

❖❖❖❖

- Identify three of your favorite places.
- For each place: List its most pleasant colors, soothing sounds, distinctive tactile sensations (gentle breeze, sun on your back, beach sand between your toes), and smells (salt air, perfume, flowers).
- Use these four elements to enhance your imagery.
- When you use an image, always recall the colors, sounds, sensations, and smells.

Lesson 36

Meditation

Sitting quietly, doing nothing.
Spring comes and the grass grows all by itself.

~ Zen poem

Meditation is another method of managing stress. It also undoes what stress does to you. It works to quiet the mind. The problem with the mind is that it will not shut up. It is always talking. In the East the chattering mind is called "monkey mind." The image evoked is one of monkeys in a tree incessantly jumping from limb to limb. Our minds, like the monkeys, quickly go from thought to thought, ranging far afield and traveling down corridors of frightful fantasy and worry. Meditation focuses thought in order to quiet the mind. Meditation elicits what Herbert Benson has labeled the "relaxation response."

Benson, a physician and researcher at Harvard Medical School, has studied the effects of stress on the body through the well-known fight or flight response. In his research, Benson identified an innate response that is the opposite of the stress reaction. Benson named it the relaxation response, and it undoes the stress reaction. The typical signs of the relaxation response are: relaxed muscles, decreased heart rate, lowered blood pressure, slower breathing, and a calm stomach. In addition, the rate of metabolism decreases while the rate of slow brain waves increases.

While the relaxation response is innate, it is elicited and not released. When facing a threat such as the squeal of brakes or your boss's criticism, the body responds with an immediate and arousing physiological reaction that quickly spreads throughout the body. This stress reaction is released with no action required by you. The relaxation response, on the other hand, must be called forth. It is elicited through your intentional actions and does not have an immediate impact on the body. The relaxation response acts more slowly than the stress reaction.

You may call forth the relaxation response when lying on a beach, sunning, and listening to the waves. You soon feel peaceful, pleasant, and tranquil. On a busy, hectic day when you need to relax, however, you probably cannot visit the beach, even if one was nearby. You may desperately need the relaxation response, but you also need it under your control. You need to know how to meditate.

The concept of meditation is simple. Just focus your mind on one thing and do not let it wander. While there are many different meditation techniques, Benson offers a practical two-step process. First, repeat to yourself a specific word, sound, prayer, or phrase, and second, passively disregard any intrusive thoughts that come while you simply return to your repetition. Follow this procedure for 10 to 20 minutes.

The word you use can be neutral such as "one," "peace," "love," "calm," or "relax." You could also choose words or phrases from a religious tradition if you so desire. Words such as "Shalom" or "Om" and phrases such as "The Lord is my shepherd" or "Hail Mary, full of grace" would work. The word or phrase chosen does not matter as long as you are comfortable with it.

The key features of this technique are to concentrate and focus the mind while disregarding any distracting thoughts that come. And, you can be sure, the distracting thoughts will come just like monkeys in a tree. All you have to do is let them come and let them go. Consistently return to your task of concentration and the relaxation response will surely follow as the stress reaction recedes. Practice this simple technique twice a day and see if your life goes better.

❖❖❖❖

- ◆ Sit quietly and pay attention to your thinking. Notice the monkey-like thoughts jumping from one thing to another.
- ◆ Try a brief meditation. Use the phrase, "I am at peace." When you inhale think to yourself, "I am ...." As you exhale think, "... at peace."
- ◆ Do this for several minutes and try not to let your mind wander.

Lesson 37

Breathing and Counting

Fear less, hope more; Whine less, breathe more.
~ Swedish Proverb

B ecause life is stressful, each day takes its toll. To handle stress, we must know how to undo what it is doing to us. While we cannot make life stress free, we can limit the effects of stress on us. Doing this requires knowing how to intentionally relax.

Please note that relaxation is not recreation, although some forms of recreation can be relaxing. Relaxation is a specific activity you can do that quickly reduces muscle tension, lowers the heart rate, lowers the blood pressure, and calms the stomach while creating a peaceful, pleasant mood. Once relaxed, a person recaptures energy and can return to a task feeling refreshed and better able to concentrate. Efficiency improves once the stress level is reduced.

While there are a variety of well-established relaxation procedures such as meditation, guided imagery, and progressive muscle relaxation, these techniques need privacy and require about 20 minutes of practice in order to yield the full benefit. During a busy day you may have neither the needed privacy nor time. It would be advantageous to have speedy means for undoing stress.

Here is a quick way to relax. It can be done just about anywhere and only takes a few minutes. All you have to do is to breathe and count to five. This is what you do. Slowly breathe in while counting to five. Count at one-second intervals such as "one-and-two-and-three-and-four-and-five." Now, hold that breath while you again slowly count to five, and finally breathe out while slowly counting to five. Repeat this procedure five times. It takes about 90 seconds. Do it as often as needed.

This method of relaxation is like a sophisticated version of counting to ten. Perhaps as a child you were told to count to ten when angry so you could have time to calm down before speaking. This counting method of relaxing helps you to slow down your breathing pattern and refocuses your attention away from stress building situations. It may work best if you have practiced other, more detailed, relaxation techniques because you will already have trained your body to know what deep relaxation is like. You can more easily recapture what you have already experienced.

An advantage of this quick procedure is that it can be done in any situation without anyone's knowledge. You can use it at work when on the phone handling a complaint. You can use it when the traffic light catches you while rushing to a meeting. It can be practiced as you walk down the hallway towards your teenager's room with the loud stereo blaring. This breathing technique helps you quickly and unobtrusively turn the tide of stress.

So, the next time life gets hectic, remember the "5 by 5" technique. Undo your stress by slowly counting to five while you inhale, holding the breath while you slowly count to five, and exhaling as you again slowly count to five. Do this five times. See if you feel more refreshed.

❖❖❖❖

◆ You can try the "5 x 5" breathing technique right now.
◆ First, pay attention to how you feel and notice any physical tension or emotional stress.
◆ Use the "5 x 5" breathing technique.
◆ Re-evaluate your tension and stress levels.
◆ Do you notice improvement?
◆ What seems to have changed?

Lesson 38

Peaceful Moments

Now and then it's good to pause in our pursuit of happiness and just be happy.

~ Guillaume Apollinaire

Each day we are offered peaceful moments in which to slow down and relax. Life tries to give us a break, but most of us miss the moment and respond with anger and frustration instead. We get upset and complain. We tell others how "bad" it is. We may even create a scene and disturb the peace of those around us. We won't just accept life's gift and relax.

For example, you are in heavy traffic rushing to a meeting, when another traffic light catches you for a long wait. Or, the elevator is taking forever no matter how many times you push the button. And once again when you switched to the short line at the grocery store, another of those "price checks" happened. You are wondering why it always happens to you. You are amazed at how it never fails. Your stress and frustration levels are rising. Life must be out to get you. What did you ever do to deserve this treatment?

At times like these, life has just slowed you down and offered you a moment to relax. Take a deep breath and enjoy it. Complaining won't change it. While the daily hassles of life can be frustrating, when seen from a proper perspective they may enliven you. Turn off your inner critical voice. Look around at the moment. You are most likely not the only one in the situation. You have not been singled out. Maybe there is a lesson here for you? What could it be? Perhaps:

- Start earlier. Allow yourself enough time so that minor delays don't matter. Stop rushing through life.
- Lighten up. Don't be so serious. A small hassle hardly ever turns into a disaster. Look for the humor in the situation.

- Unwind. Use the moment to your advantage. Learn to take all of life's delays as opportunities to relax. Practice a brief relaxation skill, such as taking slow deep breaths.
- Be more mindful of others. Focus on the people around you and talk to them.
- Practice kindness. Others may be in a hurry too. Let someone else go first.
- Become patient. Recall the prayer that says, "Lord, give me patience and give it to me *right* now!" Patience usually comes with the practice of peaceful waiting. Can you wait peacefully?

Each day you must look for life's gifts of peaceful moments. They often come in disguise. You may have to change your perspective to see them. The challenge is to learn to use that immediate sense of frustration and the familiar thought of "here we go again," as the signal to look anew at your situation. Be open to the moment and turn off that automatic response. You may be in the midst of a peaceful moment and not know it. See if you can open yourself to it. Learn to take advantage of what life offers you. Enjoy your peaceful moments.

❖❖❖❖

- Review your day and see if you can recall any peaceful moments that you may have missed?
- What could you have done to enjoy them?
- Resolve not to miss your next peaceful moment.

Lesson 39

The Healing Power of Nature

*Climb the mountains and get their good tidings; nature's peace
will flow into you as sunshine into flowers; the winds will blow
their freshness into you and the storms their energy, and cares
will drop off like autumn leaves.*

~ John Muir

Prison inmates whose cellblock windows overlook a garden
have a better frame of mind than those who can only see a brick
wall. You may not be in prison but looking at nature can help you.
The next time you are having a bad day and feeling stressed out, try
looking out a window. What you see may calm you down and
improve your mood.

Research has found that hospital patients with courtyard rooms
viewing plants, flowers, and greenery are discharged one day earlier than those without such a view. These same patients also require
less pain medication. Furthermore, office workers with windows
overlooking trees and landscapes are more productive than those
workers without windows.

It is not just having a window but what is seen that is important.
Some signs of vegetation are needed. We need to see something
green. It even helps to have simulated views of nature. Photographs
and paintings of natural settings help to relieve the boredom of
people in confined settings.

We Americans spend about 84 percent of our time indoors with
locked windows, climate controlled air, and fluorescent lighting.
So, even better than looking out a window is to go outside. Take a
break. Go on a short walk. Look at the sky, smell the flowers, feel
the ground under your feet. If you can't take a walk, stand in the
doorway and feel the heat of the sun, the cool of a breeze, or the
mist of the rain. Let nature rejuvenate you.

Also, you can bring nature inside. Put a plant or fresh flowers in your office. Use an arrangement of seashells from your vacation or stones that you picked up on a hike as a reminder of a peaceful time. Let a desktop waterfall bring the soothing sounds of flowing water. Place a bird feeder outside your window. Bring nature to you.

Being in natural settings has always been relaxing and refreshing, but in modern life we have isolated ourselves from these experiences. We have lost our connection with Mother Nature. We human beings were at one time always immersed in natural settings. Often it was peaceful, but sometimes it was threatening; so, we tried to control it with barriers such as fences, walls, and dams. In trying to protect ourselves from the harmful impact of uncontrolled nature, we have also robbed ourselves of its healing influence.

It is time to reconnect with nature and to recognize that nature now needs our protection. We must become its guardians so that when we look out the window there will be something natural and beautiful to observe, and we can relax and refresh ourselves in the seeing.

If your life is stressful, find a window through which you can look and discover what you can see. Hopefully, it will be something green and growing.

❖❖❖❖

- ◆ Have you enjoyed nature today?
- ◆ Can you take a walk now?
- ◆ Could you watch the sunrise or sunset?
- ◆ Maybe you can buy yourself some flowers.

Lesson 40

Sadder than Sad: Depression

When I hear somebody sigh that "Life is hard," I am always tempted to ask, "Compared to what?

~ Sidney J. Harris

Life is filled with a variety of experiences, and depending upon circumstances, it is appropriate to be feeling any number of positive and negative emotions. Some of these emotional states include excitement, frustration, fear, happiness, anger, sadness, and joy. All of these feelings are normal reactions to specific life events. Even when they are experienced as unpleasant, they are just normal reactions.

These normal emotions, however, can intensify into abnormal states if they become an overreaction to circumstances. It is even possible to become too happy and create a problem. When you are too happy, your energy level rises, and you can be on the go non-stop. You can work all day and clean the house all night. Everything seems possible. You make grand plans and quick decisions based on little data. Your friends may suggest that you are losing control, but you don't understand what they could possibly mean. Everything seems great to you. You are spiraling into a manic state but cannot see it until everything comes crashing down. You are happier than happy, and you have a problem.

On the other hand, if a store clerk is rude, you may respond with normal irritation and complain to the manager. However, if your irritation grows and escalates into anger and rage, you may create such a scene that you become the rude and obnoxious person. You are angrier than angry and headed toward trouble.

In a similar manner, experiencing a loss may make you sad, but if the sadness becomes out of proportion to the event, you fall into depression. Sadness is normal, but depression is not. Depression differs from sadness in its intensity, frequency, and duration.

- Intensity - While the event would make most people sad, you respond with a much deeper level of sadness. It is too intense. Your sadness moves outside the normal range of response.
- Frequency - Your sadness may not be out of proportion, but it is recurrent. You seem to get over it, and then it comes back. This repetitive cycle becomes a pattern in your life.
- Duration - Your sadness comes, and it stays and stays. The sadness lasts much longer than it does for most other people in similar circumstances.

Any one or a combination of these three factors can result in depression. Depression is when you have become sadder than sad.

A curious feature of depression is that it is possible to be depressed and not know it. You may never describe yourself as depressed or even sad. You may have no awareness of sadness, but you can still be depressed. Many depressed people make their way to the physician's office thinking that they are ill only to be told that depression is involved. The syndrome of depression consists of many different symptoms, and sadness is but one of them.

Frequently, people mask their feelings and hide them not only from others, but from themselves as well. If you know how to put on a "happy face" when you are feeling down, you know how to do this. If you can smile while feeling bad, others may think that you are all right. If you are very good at this hiding of emotion, you may also fool yourself. You may mask your depression behind a smile.

How do you know if you are depressed? What are the symptoms? The table below lists the major signs of depression. Look it over and see how you are doing. The presence and intensity of these symptoms in your life determine whether or not you are depressed.

Symptoms of Depression

◆ Sadness	◆ Discouragement
◆ Sense of failure	◆ Feeling punished
◆ Disappointment	◆ Self-criticism
◆ Guilt feelings	◆ Suicidal thoughts
◆ Lack of energy	◆ Crying spells
◆ Irritation	◆ Insomnia
◆ Poor appetite	◆ Weight loss
◆ Health concerns	◆ Obsessive worry
◆ Loss of interest in sex	◆ Loss of motivation
◆ Loss of social interest	◆ Difficulty making decisions

If you think you are depressed, it is a good idea to measure the symptoms you have. Take the following depression test and see how you are doing. Measuring depression is like getting on the scales before you go on a diet. When dieting you should weigh yourself before starting so that when you weigh again, you can tell if you are making progress.

If you are depressed, knowing your initial level of depression is helpful when you begin working to lower it. You can use your initial depression score to track your progress over time. As you work on the issues of depression, your score should begin to go down as a sign of improvement.

❖❖❖

Test for Depression

As you fill out the questionnaire, read each item and mark the answer that best reflects how you have been feeling during the past few days. Make sure you choose one answer for each of the twelve statements. If in doubt, make your best guess. **Do not leave any items unanswered.** To get your score when you finish, add up all of the numbers that you chose. Go to page 184 for the results.

Question 1

I feel miserable and sad most of the time.

0 No, not at all.
1 No, not much.
2 Yes, sometimes.
3 Yes, definitely.

Question 2

I find it difficult to do the things I used to do.

0 No, not at all.
1 No, not much.
2 Yes, sometimes.
3 Yes, definitely.

Question 3

I get very frightened or panicky for no good reason.

0 No, not at all.
1 No, not much.
2 Yes, sometimes.
3 Yes, definitely.

Question 4

I am restless and can't keep still.

0 No, not at all.
1 No, not much.
2 Yes, sometimes.
3 Yes, definitely.

Question 5

I have lost the joyfulness I had.

0 No, not at all.
1 No, not much.
2 Yes, sometimes.
3 Yes, definitely.

Question 6

I have crying spells.

0 No, not at all.
1 No, not much.
2 Yes, sometimes.
3 Yes, definitely.

Question 7

I need medication in order to sleep.

0 No, not at all.
1 No, not much.
2 Yes, sometimes.
3 Yes, definitely.

Question 8

I feel anxious when I go out of the house alone.

0 No, not at all.
1 No, not much.
2 Yes, sometimes.
3 Yes, definitely.

Question 9

I have lost interest in things.

0 No, not at all.
1 No, not much.
2 Yes, sometimes.
3 Yes, definitely.

Question 10

I wake up early in the morning and cannot go back to sleep.

0 No, not at all.
1 No, not much.
2 Yes, sometimes.
3 Yes, definitely.

Question 11

I am more irritable than usual.

0 No, not at all.
1 No, not much.
2 Yes, sometimes.
3 Yes, definitely.

Question 12

I get tired for no reason.

0 No, not at all.
1 No, not much.
2 Yes, sometimes.
3 Yes, definitely.

◆ Add up all of the numbers that you chose to get your score.
◆ Go to page 184 for the results.

(This test is not meant to replace a clinical assessment but to help you judge how you are doing. If you score as depressed, you may want to consider seeking counseling.)

Lesson 41

Depression and Its Causes

Unhappiness indicates wrong thinking, just as ill health indicates a bad regimen.

~ Paul Bourge

What is the cause of depression? While no single answer exists, several possible explanations are available, and more than one possibility can be involved at the same time.

Physiology

Sometimes depression is referred to as a "biological depression," meaning that a person is depressed because of a biochemical imbalance of some sort. Usually, this involves the brain and a variety of neurotransmitters, chemicals that help different areas of the brain communicate. If these chemicals are low in quantity, miscommunication can occur, and depression may be the result.

The process is similar to diabetes in which a physical malfunction of the pancreas results in the need for a medication to correct the sugar imbalance in the blood. Insulin is often required to return the body to a state of equilibrium. Usually continued medication is required to enable living a normal life. Also, lifestyle changes often must be made, such as adopting a new diet, following an exercise program, and learning to manage stress.

If there is a biochemical component to your depression, you may need medication to help you overcome it. When in a deep depression, pharmaceuticals can help "jump start" the recovery process; so, you can then do the other needed work for healing.

Some people, but not all, have significant biochemical components to their depression. However, other factors can be involved as well.

Change and Stress

Some people become depressed when overwhelmed by change and stress. As said earlier, we live in a time of rapidly increasing change, and the requirements of adaptation are difficult. Too many demands in too short a time may overburden some people. Stress begins wearing them out, and a loss of resiliency results. As their energy level decreases, these people begin to isolate themselves by pulling away from others. They no longer bounce back from adversity. Moods of gloom and pessimism appear. Motivation is lost. Depression sets in.

Learning

Sometimes we learn to be depressed. People learn what they live with. If you grew up in a family where everyone was angry, you would think anger was normal. If you were raised in an anxious family, anxiety would seem the norm. Similarly, in a family where others were depressed, you might come to think that such moods were routine. You would learn a social role with a depressed approach to life.

On the other hand, it might be that your family was normal, but busy. If as a child you were playing quietly in your room by yourself, your parents might think, "Good. Don't disturb her. Let her play." In essence, they would ignore you when you were being good. Later, if you were sad and crying because your toy had broken, your parents might rush over to see what was wrong. The result is that you received attention and were rewarded for being upset. Whether meaning to or not, your parents taught you a rule about life in your family. *To get attention you must be in distress.* This lesson could be the first step in learning a lifestyle of depression as attention-getting behavior, especially if there are also other family members who have similar behavior patterns, perhaps a mother or a sister who is ill and gets attention for being sick.

Learning that attention only comes when you feel bad or down can be a stepping stone to depression.

Thinking

Many people think themselves into depression. It is easy to do. All that is required is that you know how to worry. With worry, you take any small problem and think about it as you imagine what might go wrong and how terrible it will be. Pretty soon you will have a big problem. This problem is one that you have created, and it exists primarily in your imagination. However, if you forget that you have intensified the problem by adding to it, you take it for "the reality" of your situation. If you develop a habit of negative thinking and always make things worse than they are, you can lead yourself down the road to depression.

A Universal Pathway

There are at least these four pathways to depression: physiology, stress, learning, and thinking. They often act together. If you are depressed, you need to evaluate all of four of these factors in your life. In making your evaluation, you will most likely find that no matter what else is going on, thinking is always involved. Thinking is a universal pathway to depression. Regardless of what the other causes of depression may contribute, thinking, especially negative thinking, always plays some role and can always make matters worse.

- ◆ Even if you are depressed because of a biochemical imbalance, you will continue to think and interpret your life experiences.
- ◆ If you have too much stress, you will certainly think about the stressful events.
- ◆ If you learned to be depressed, your learned pattern of thinking will maintain it.

Thinking is always occurring, and plays a fundamental role in creating not only depression, but all of your other emotions as well. However, you can control your thinking. You can choose what you tell yourself. Learn to control the pathway of thinking, and you will have influence over your moods and behavior.

- How does thinking influence your moods? Is it for better or worse?
- How can your thinking affect your physical functioning? Can you think yourself into an upset stomach?
- How does your thinking affect your stress level?
- What kind of a thinking style did you learn as a child? Were you more optimistic or pessimistic?

Lesson 42

The ABC's of Life

The greatest discovery of my generation is that human beings can alter their lives by altering their attitudes of mind.

~ William James

Our minds work nonstop. Thinking is always occurring, and it plays a fundamental role in the creation of our emotions. Understanding how our thinking creates our moods and influences our behavior is an area of cognitive psychology. Trying to change our thinking to improve our moods and behavior is cognitive therapy. Cognitive therapy provides a good model for self-help.

One of the easiest cognitive therapy approaches to understand is that of Rational Emotive Therapy (RET) as developed by Albert Ellis. RET tells us about the ABC's of emotional life. It is practical and easy to apply.

- "A" stands for "Actual Event" and represents what happens to you in life.
- "B" stands for a "Belief" about what happened.
- "C" stands for the "Consequence" of the event on mood and behavior.

In life, it appears that events happen and affect both moods and behavior. It seems that A (an event) causes C (a consequence). So, if a friend breaks your trust, you may be hurt and depressed. You may tell someone that your friend has ruined your life and made you miserable. In order to be hurt and depressed, however, you must have a belief or interpretation about what happened. You must be thinking in a certain way. It is your belief or thinking that is creating your reaction. You might be thinking, "It is horrible. It is terrible. I have been betrayed. I'll never trust again."

A	B	C
Actual Event	**Belief**	**Consequence**
Trust is broken	**"It is horrible and terrible."**	**Hurt and depressed**

Your beliefs create the consequence. Change the belief and the consequence will change. What else could you tell yourself? What might be a more realistic assessment of the event?

You could think, "This is tough, and I don't like it, but I am glad that I found out now rather than later. I made a mistake, but I can learn from it. I can get through it." Your reaction will be one of hurt and disappointment, which is a more realistic response to the situation. You will not fall into a state of depression and misery. You will feel more in control and better able to cope.

A	B	C
Actual Event	**Belief**	**Consequence**
Trust is broken	**"It is tough, but at least I found out now. I can get through it."**	**Hurt and disappointed**

Changing your belief changes the consequence. Your belief will be evident in the inner dialogue that you have with yourself. It is in the Voice of Conscience that talks to you about life.

This Voice is the one that often speaks up when you look in the mirror or get on the scales. It can talk you into a lot of trouble. Learn to pay attention to this inner voice and be sure that it is realistic. Don't fall into a negative pattern of worry or self-criticism that can only make matters worse. Realistic thinking will lead to realistic consequences over which you have a sense of control.

When you do find a negative belief, you must challenge it. You do this with step "D" of the ABC model. "D" stands for "Dispute." Dispute means that once you have identified a negative or irrational belief, you challenge it. You dispute it. You create a more realistic view and a more supportive inner dialogue.

A	B	C
Actual Event	**Belief**	**Consequence**
Trust is broken	**"It is horrible and terrible. I will never get over it."**	**Hurt and depressed and feeling helpless.**

D	E
Dispute	**(new) Effect**
"It is tough but at least I found out now. I can get through it."	**Hurt and disappointed but still in control.**

A new dialogue leads to "E" which stands for "Effect"—a (new) Effect. The result of a different belief is a different reaction. The same event now leads to different emotions and behavior. With a new dialogue you regain control of your life.

Remember the ABC's of emotional life. Always be sure you evaluate your self-talk, and don't talk yourself into more trouble than you need. Using your ABC's will help you to change your thinking and emotions and make life go better.

❖❖❖❖

- The next time you are sad or in a bad mood, use the ABC model.
- When you become aware of negative consequences, "C," and are feeling bad, ask yourself, "What have I been thinking?" Don't ask, "Who made me feel this way?"
- You need to identify "A," the event, but then focus on how you have been interpreting it.
- See if you can change your belief, "B," so you get a different reaction.

Lesson 43

The Skill of Bouncing Back

*Have a variety of interests... These interests relax the mind and
lessen tension on the nervous system. People with many interests live, not only longest, but happiest.*

~ George Matthew Allen

R esiliency is the ability to bounce back from the ups and downs
of life. How resilient are you? How resilient you are today
depends on how you were taking care of your resiliency resources
yesterday. Resiliency is the energy that allows you to enrich life. It
is something we all have. We are born with resiliency, but we can
lose it.

Your resiliency is like a lake and a dam that make up a reservoir. All of the water in the lake behind the dam represents your life
energy. You use this energy to handle the daily stresses and strains
of life. Whenever change or stress enters your life, the floodgates
of the dam open and some energy flows out into the world to help
you cope. If the stress is small, the floodgates open just a little and
some energy flows out. With a bigger stress or a series of stresses,
the gates open wider and more energy flows away. If it is a major
crisis or chronic, continual stress and change, then the gates open
very, very wide, and all of your energy can flow out into the world.
The lakebed is now dry, and you have no energy left.

What is this loss of energy like? Two main words are used to
describe it. In the workplace, it is called "burnout" and means that
you have done the job just a little too long and cannot do it anymore. Outside of the work setting, this loss of energy is called
"depression." In either case you have lost energy and motivation.
You have no "get up and go" left and experience a general lack of
interest in both people and tasks. Sadness, irritation, and frustration

are present, making you hard to live with—both for yourself and for others.

Your challenge, when you give out of resiliency, is to put some energy back into the reservoir. In fact, you should have been refilling it all the time. What can do you do to keep it full? The answer is simple. Just do something that you enjoy, and do it every day. Have some fun each day, and you will be refilling the resiliency reservoir.

Having fun every day sounds simple, and it is; however, it is not easy. Simple and easy are not the same. Confirm this for yourself by taking a resiliency test. Get a pencil and a sheet of paper and quickly make an "Enjoyable Things List" of 20 things you like to do. Anything at all, as long as you enjoy it. (You can find an example of an Enjoyable Things List in Appendix C on page 186.)

If you are like most people, you will be shocked to find that you start running out of items by the time you reach number 10. When you can hardly think of 10 fun things, it is rather sad and pathetic because life offers endless possibilities for enjoyment. If you have only a limited repertoire of fun from which to choose, it is like going to a restaurant and being given a menu with only three items and finding that you hate all three. You will either have to do without or suffer through something you don't like. If you do not have a long list of things you like to do, you have a limited menu for fun.

Furthermore, suppose that all the items on your list require a bright sunny day, and today it is raining. With no rainy day activities, there is no fun for you today. Not only should you have a long list of things you enjoy, but you must also add variety to the list if you want to be a more resilient person.

Once you have your Enjoyable Things List, you must test it. Your list may not be doing you any good. Read each item and put the letter "W" by each one you have actually done in the last week.

Now, suppose that you did about 80 percent of the things on your list, and were asked how life was going. What would the answer be? Most likely that life is great. What if you did about 45 percent of the items? How will life look? Probably, life is okay. If you only did 20 percent of the things you enjoy, life may be dull, and if you did none of the things on your list, life will be looking very dreary and sad. If you have had no fun in the past week, you may be in the midst of burnout or in a depression with accompanying low levels of energy and motivation.

In life, the more enjoyable things that you are doing, the better your experience of life will be. The more fun things you are doing, the more energy you will have. If you are not doing things you enjoy every day, you are not replenishing your resiliency energy. You are heading towards burnout or depression.

Here is Resiliency Secret Number 1: *Do something you enjoy every day.* Have fun every day, and do it whether you feel like it or not. How you feel is not important, but what you do is. Have fun on purpose. Your energy will increase, and life will go better.

❖❖❖❖

- What have you already done for fun today?
- What are you looking forward to doing next?
- Can you have fun right now?

Lesson 44

Waiting for a Miracle

You are what you think. You are what you go for. You are what you do!

~ Bob Richards

We should all be taught not to wait for inspiration to start a thing. Action always generates inspiration. Inspiration seldom generates action.

~ Frank Tibolt

Have you ever said to someone, "I don't feel like it?" Maybe you were asked to got to a movie, go out to eat, or do an unpleasant task, but you say, "I don't feel like it." Most of us have said this from time to time.

When your mood is low and you are feeling burnt-out or depressed, someone could choose a favorite activity from your Enjoyable Things List, invite you to do it, and offer to pay for it, but you will always have the same answer. You say, "No. I don't feel like it."

Saying, "I don't feel like it," you have quickly summed up your philosophy for life, for how life works. You are saying that life is like this. In life you don't do things until...until when? Well, until you feel like it.

Now, the question to consider is this: How long will it take you to feel like it? You might sit and wait a few minutes and suddenly feel like it. You might sit for an hour as you wait to feel like it. Maybe, a few hours? A day? A week? A month? Maybe a year?

The problem is that when you are waiting to feel like it, you are waiting on the "M" Word to strike in your life. What is the word starting with "M" that you are waiting on? People often answer with, "Motivation." Good try, but that is not it. It is also not

"Money" or "Mood." It is not "Medication." It is not "Mama" or "Mother" to make you do it.

The "M" word is "Miracle." You are waiting on a miracle. Why is it a miracle? It is a miracle because you want to sit there doing absolutely nothing until, suddenly, something from outside strikes you, fills you with energy, motivation, ambition, and desire, and makes you want to enjoy something without you doing anything but sitting there. What do we call this strategy? We call it waiting for a miracle. It is not the best plan for life. You don't wait for a miracle. You must make the miracle.

You can do this once you know what comes first in life: motivation or action? Most people say it is motivation, but the good news is that the answer is *action*. If you *are* motivated, well and good because you get up and do it, but what if you are not motivated? Now you are back to waiting on a miracle. The secret of making a miracle is to act first and allow the motivation to follow.

Such miracles happen all the time. For example, just recall when you were asked to go somewhere that you did not want to go. I mean, you *really* did not want to go. Maybe it was to the ballet, a family reunion, or a mud-wrestling match. However, someone begged, pleaded, or even threatened until you reluctantly agreed. You agreed only after secretly having vowed to make them miserable the whole time; after all, they would have to pay for this. A short time after you arrived, however, and much to your surprise, you began having fun. In fact, you had a great time. It was the best time in months.

Now, what was your motivation for going? None! You did not feel like going, but you took action anyway. You went. By acting you placed yourself in the circumstances where the motivation could follow. Motivation and energy caught up with you. So, the secret to motivation is, "Just do it." Do it whether you feel like it or not. Act first and create the motivation. Create your own energy.

This is especially true for things you usually enjoy. While it seems that you would just do them because they are fun, often you choose not to do so. Let's say you had planned on going out to a movie with friends, but you had a hard day at work. Now that you are at home, you *just don't feel like it.* If you choose not to go, do you start to feel better right away? No! Now you have two problems. You not only had a bad day, but you are also angry because you did not get to do what you had planned to do. (Of course, don't forget you chose not to do it.) Go to the movie anyway. Do whatever you had planned. Allow the energy to catch up with you. Act first. Energy and motivation will follow.

The next time you hear yourself saying, "I don't feel like it," call a time out. Remind yourself that you are choosing to wait for a miracle. Choose to make the miracle instead. Take action. Do whatever it is, whether you feel like it or not. Create your own motivation. Raise your energy level.

❖❖❖❖

- What fun things can you make yourself do today that will give you energy?
- What fun things did you make yourself do in the past week?
- Can you identify lost opportunities when taking action would have helped raise your resiliency level?

Lesson 45

The Importance of Accomplishment

Look at a day when you are supremely satisfied at the end. It's not a day when you lounge around doing nothing; it's when you've had everything to do, and you've done it.

~ Margaret Thatcher

Here is another resiliency secret. Return to your Enjoyable Things List. Look it over. It should be composed of two major categories. One category will be those things that you like to do because they are fun. This is why you enjoy them. It may include activities, such as going to a movie or visiting with friends. The other category will consist of things that are not fun but which you still enjoy. You enjoy them for a different reason.

This second category has items like cleaning the toilet. This is certainly not much fun, but when you finish you feel good. You feel good because when you stand back and look at the sparkling, shiny-clean toilet bowl, you have a sense of satisfaction at getting something done. You feel a sense of accomplishment. Each day you need to engage in some activities that provide this sense of accomplishment. Such activities help to make life meaningful and worthwhile because they replenish your resiliency reservoir of life energy.

Many potentially unpleasant tasks provide a sense of accomplishment. Things like: organizing a closet, mopping a floor, or mowing the grass. Maybe, even going to work. Hopefully, your job does give you the satisfaction of getting something done.

Unfortunately, some days at work do not go well, and you may leave the office feeling frustrated, and that the day was wasted. Nothing was achieved. When you come home at the end of this kind of day, you now know what to do. You know Resiliency Secret

Number 2. What is the first thing you should do when you get home? That's right. *Immediately go clean the toilet!* You will have a sense of accomplishment. Life is already going better. The only thing left to do is to a have fun before bedtime, and you will have had a good day.

Life will challenge your resiliency resources every day. You must replenish them every day by taking time to do things you enjoy. Each night when going to sleep, ask yourself two questions. First: "Did I have any fun today?" The answer should be yes to at least one thing. Second: "Did I get anything done today?" Again, the answer should be yes to at least one thing. If you can answer both questions positively, you have had a good day and are well on the road to resiliency. If you can answer each question with more than one thing you have done, so much the better.

Every day do something you enjoy. In fact, do several things you enjoy, and remember that the things you enjoy also include those activities that provide a sense of accomplishment. The more you do what you enjoy, the more resiliency you create, and the more energy you will have to invest in life.

❖❖❖❖

- What have you already accomplished today?
- What do you plan to accomplish?
- What could you do right now?
- What additional activities of accomplishment can you add to your Enjoyable Things List?

Lesson 46

Fun on the Run

Never put off until tomorrow what you can do today because if you enjoy it today, you can do it again tomorrow.

~ Anonymous

How quickly can you have fun? On a day not going well and when your resiliency resources are running low, how fast can you replenish them? How quickly can you get your energy back? The speed of your bouncing back will depend upon the variety of the items on your Enjoyable Things List. How many of the items that you listed take planning, and how many can be immediately done?

Find out by reading over your list and putting the letter "P" (for planning) by each item that takes you more than 15 minutes just to get ready to do it. For example, I like going to the movies, but it takes me more than 15 minutes just to drive across town to the theater. For me, moviegoing requires some planning. Is this true for you? What is your list like?

When you finish going over your list, if you have a lot of "Ps", you are probably well organized. You can have fun on schedule, and scheduling fun is needed. It is important to plan for enjoyable things such as an upcoming European vacation, a ski trip, or a long awaited concert of a favorite performer. These activities provide high quality fun, moreover, you always get to enjoy them three times. You enjoy the excited anticipation as you plan for them; you enjoy the actual experience; you enjoy recalling what it was like as you tell others about it. We certainly need planned fun in our lives. It is very important.

Planned events, however, are in the future. What if you need fun today? Suppose your energy is low right now? What simple and spontaneous things can you do? These things should be the items on your list that do not have a "P" beside them. They might include:

♦ Having a cup of coffee.
♦ Reading the newspaper.
♦ Listening to music.
♦ Singing a song.
♦ Petting a dog or cat.
♦ Watching a sunset.
♦ Giving a hug.
♦ Taking a walk.
♦ Reading a book.

These and many more simple pleasures can enliven life while recapturing your energy. They can be quickly and easily done in almost any setting. On a hectic day, these spontaneous things are your best bet for enhancing your resiliency.

To be effective, however, these more simple, unplanned items must be done with mindfulness. You must be aware of them as you do them. A good example is taking a hot shower. Many people report this to be a rejuvenating morning activity that gets their day off to a good start. If you take a shower, however, and your mind is focused on a problem, it does not truly benefit you. All the shower does is get you clean. It does not build resilience because you were not really there. In order to get the benefit of such a simple pleasure as a hot shower, you must be fully present. You must be actively enjoying it by thinking about how good that hot water feels at the moment. Do this, and you will become clean—and resilient.

Similarly, if you pet your dog while worrying about a problem, your dog gets some benefit, but you do not. Again, you were not present.

It is important to become aware that no single day is totally bad. All days, even bad ones, have their small pleasures such as eating a snack, hearing a bird sing, or just taking a slow deep breath.

Such simple things can enliven life, if you will only *notice and appreciate them.* Appreciating them is important. Be careful not to discount simple, ordinary pleasures because if you do so, you rob yourself of resilience.

It is easy to say of a simple pleasure that it doesn't count because *"Everyone does that."* This may be true. Everyone does do it, but the problem is that not everyone appreciates it. Learn to appreciate the small things. Becoming more mindful of your experience creates energy and adds to life's enjoyment. It also adds to your resiliency reservoir, the container of your life energy. Learn to be grateful for simple pleasures.

❖❖❖❖

◆ What simple pleasures have you enjoyed today?
◆ Recall any simple pleasures you may have overlooked. Did you have fun and not know it?
◆ What plans are you making for fun? What do you have planned for tonight? This weekend? Next month? Next summer?

Lesson 47

Fun Alone and Fun Together

*I am now quite cured of seeking pleasure in society, be it coun-
try or town. A sensible man ought to find sufficient company in
himself.* ~ Emily Bronte

Man absolutely cannot live by himself. ~ Erich Fromm

Can you have fun alone or do you do better with others around?
Check your Enjoyable Things List and see what it says. Read
the items and put the letter "A" by each one that you usually do
alone. When finished, look for a pattern.

Do you have a lot of "A's?" If so, there is good news and bad
news. The good news is that you can entertain yourself. You can
have fun alone and may even enjoy being alone. The bad news is
that you may withdraw from others and isolate yourself. You may
be eliminating enlivening social activities from your life. Some
high quality, energetic fun comes from relationships, and such fun
greatly adds to your resiliency resources. Don't eliminate these
options from your life. Don't be too much of a loner.

Suppose that you have only a few "A's" on your list. What does
this mean? Again, there is good and bad news. The good news is
that you are sociable, outgoing, and enjoy being with people. The
bad news is that you may actually depend upon other people to
entertain you, and when left alone have no resources for enjoyment.
You may sink into despair when by yourself with no one to provide
a distraction.

To be a resilient person, you need to be able to have fun alone
and with others. A balance is needed. You need the skills and
options of choice to appreciate and enjoy solitude, but the willingness to engage with others in social activity. If there is imbalance,
how can you correct it?

If you derive joy from only a few of the activities that you do alone, you must intentionally add more enjoyable solitary items to your list. Find out what your friends are doing when they are alone (perhaps reading, gardening, or meditating) and give it a try for yourself. Schedule time alone and practice having fun. Explore any resistances you encounter. How did you become this way? Was there a time when you liked to be alone? If so, how did you lose it? See if you can recapture the pleasure of being alone.

If you avoid being with others, you must begin to seek out more social opportunities. When invited to participate in a group activity, such as a party, you must accept, even though you would rather not. You can choose to intentionally challenge yourself by inviting others to participate with you. Even though it is uncomfortable, throw a dinner party. Learn to have fun with others in spite of yourself.

The more readily you can have fun alone, and the more often you can enjoy the company of others, the greater your resiliency resources will be.

❖❖❖❖

- ◆ What have you already enjoyed alone today?
- ◆ What plans do you have for solitary activity?
- ◆ Have you already had fun with others?
- ◆ What are your plans for being with people this week?

Lesson 48

The Cost of Having Fun

Money is better than poverty, if only for financial reasons.
~ Woody Allen

The only wealth is life.
~Henry David Thoreau

As we have seen resiliency is the ability to bounce back from the ups and downs of life. Life will use up your resiliency energy if you do not do something to replenish it. Your Enjoyable Things List can guide you in the daily renewal of resiliency. Having already evaluated these items in several ways, try one more. Read over your list of the things you enjoy and put a dollar sign ($) by each one that costs you more than $15 each time you do it.

You are trying to find out how much it costs you to have fun. When you finish, if nothing but dollar signs are on your list you are reporting that you can't have fun without spending money. If this is true, you best have a lot of money or hope to win the lottery soon.

What happens if you have no money or just don't want to spend it? There will be no fun for you, unless you have some items on your list that are free.

Earlier you determined how much planning you had to do in order to enjoy something by placing the letter "P" beside the items on your Enjoyable Things List that required scheduling. A "P" is usually accompanied by a "$." These items are the ones that cost you, and while they are often a good investment for the return in resiliency they bring, you also need some free things to do.

All the items on your list without a "P" are usually free. Check and see if this is true for you. Are these things the ones you can do to have free or low-cost fun? Often they will be simple pleasures that can be quickly done. They might include a walk in a park, a visit with a friend, or perhaps just enjoying the sound of the rain outside your window.

Don't rely on money for fun. Be sure that your resiliency list has plenty of free items and practice them as often as you can. Build some of these activities into your life every day.

❖❖❖❖

◆ Think of five free things you can do for fun.
◆ Do one of them. Now!

Lesson 49

Practicing Deviancy

Mix a little foolishness with your serious plans: it's lovely to be silly at the right moment.   ~ Horace

The less routine the more life.   ~ Amos Bronson Alcott

Have you been deviant today? Have you broken any rules? You can enliven your life by practicing deviancy and learning to be different.

All of us develop patterns of routine that organize and structure our day. Routine is helpful, but with the passage of time a routine can become rigid. We have rules that we live by, and we are often reluctant to change them. A danger is that, over time, the rules and routine may become a rut of monotony, and we will be stuck in a pattern of living that is emotionally deadening. Our habitual routine may provide a set of blinders to a more exciting and challenging life.

To break out of routine, you can be deviant. You can do something different on purpose. It may be as simple as changing the way you drive to work. Do you take the same route every day? How long have you done so? Do you ever vary it or do you just see the same scenery over and over? Try this: Tomorrow, go a different way. Leave earlier if you have to. See something different. Take the scenic route. Be open to the experience and see if it brightens your day. Do the same thing on your way home. Take a different road— the one less traveled by you. See if variety enriches your life.

Here are some other ways to practice deviancy:

- Wear a new color. Make it bright.
- Buy a bold tie.
- Mismatch your socks and see if anyone notices.

- Eat a new food. Something exotic.
- Go to a movie in the middle of the day.
- Change your hairstyle.
- Send yourself flowers.
- Run barefoot through a park.
- Skip instead of walk.

To change a routine, you must recognize that you have one. Can you identify your routines? What do you do day after day? Do you have a morning routine? A bedtime routine? Exercise routine? What about the weekends? Do you always do the same thing?

When you find a routine, ask yourself these questions:

- Why do I do this?
- Did I choose it or just fall into it?
- Do I like it?
- Is it helpful?
- Can I change it?

Evaluate your routines and determine if they are useful or just habits. If they don't seem useful, challenge them. Learn to be deviant on purpose. Put variety into your day. For a healthier and happier life, be sure to bring some deviancy into your life every day. Break out of your routines.

❖❖❖❖

- Identify one of your routines.
- Brainstorm five ways to challenge it.
- For the next five days, do it differently each day.
- See which way you like best.

Part Three:

Lessons for Growing:
Reaching for Wholeness

L ife always challenges us to grow towards our full potential. Such challenges often come through confrontations with the natural process of change. Nothing stays the same. Learning to understand and anticipate the repeating cycle of change aids us on the journey towards wholeness. Furthermore, knowing when to let go, when to forgive, when to quit, and when to take a risk are important steps along the way. Eventually, we must learn to love and accept, first ourselves and then others. Also, on the journey towards wholeness, we have the possibility of healing. Healing involves finding a spiritual center that provides our lives with a deep sense of meaning and purpose.

The *Lessons* of Part Three focus on our responsibility for making choices that challenge the limiting assumptions we have about who we are. The more often we confront our assumptions, the more fully we can engage the process of becoming the people we were meant to be.

❖❖❖❖

Lesson 50

A Riddle for Change

I was seldom able to see an opportunity until it had ceased to be one.

~ Mark Twain

L ife is full of change. It has always been so. Now, however, computers and the Internet speed information around the world so quickly that change is extraordinarily fast. To effectively manage change, you must anticipate what is coming so you can prepare. If caught by surprise, you may be in danger of being over-whelmed. A child's riddle helps explain the modern challenge of coping with change.

Once there was a beautiful lake in the middle of a small village that brought delight to everyone who visited it. The water was cool, crystal clear, and wonderfully refreshing for swimmers. Canoes and rowboats provided hours of pleasant relaxation, and fishing was always exciting because of the possibility of catching the "big one" that was known to inhabit the waters.

One day there appeared in the lake a single, small lily pad. No one noticed. The next day there were two lily pads, and no one noticed. The lily pads continued doubling every day until at the end of thirty days the lake was choked full of the green growth. The question—on what day was the lake half full? The answer is on the 29th day.

On the 29th day, you could go swimming if you desired. You could also go boating, and you might catch a fish, but on the very next day the lake is dying. There is no possibility of swimming, boating, or fishing.

Suppose that on the 29th day you noticed that the lily pads were doubling. What could you do? Nothing! It is much too late to take any corrective action. If you had recognized the problem earlier, perhaps on the third or fourth day, you could have done something, but not now.

What is the lesson of the riddle? Be vigilant. Don't let unexpected change overwhelm you. In the turbulence of change, things can creep up on you. Pay close attention to what is going on around you at all times. *Notice when the lily pads begin to double.*

To be prepared for change you must be *proactive.* You must always be looking ahead to see what is coming and be ready for quick action. Don't expect things to stay the same. Don't put your head in the sand, and when you see signs of change, do something. Don't just hope it will simply go away.

To be proactive you must practice these five steps as you begin anticipating change:

- Be observant and look for trends.
- Actively seek new information from a variety of sources.
- Be open to new possibilities, and don't fall into a rut of routine expectation.
- Listen to your intuition. Your gut instinct may give you a warning.
- Take action, even if it is risky. It may be more risky to stay the same.

If you know what is coming far enough in advance, you can prepare. You may not like it, but you can get ready. Whether it is a career change, acknowledging difficulty in a relationship, or confronting a significant loss, you *will* be ready when the time comes. You will have thought through different options and have made plans. When you see change on the horizon and prepare for it, you can capitalize on the opportunity that may be coming and not be overwhelmed by an unanticipated crisis.

Don't wait until it is too late to act. Always look ahead. Don't become complacent. Keep an eye on the lake. Watch the lily pads.

- ◆ Have any recent changes caught you off guard?
- ◆ In retrospect, were there early warning signs?
- ◆ If so, how did you overlook them?
- ◆ What did you learn about the need to anticipate change?
- ◆ How can you practice being more proactive?

Lesson 51

The Wheel of Life and the Four Phases of Change

Because things are the way they are, things will not stay the way they are.

~ Bertolt Brecht

The Wheel of Life is the Medieval model of change. It describes the phases and emotions of the change process. During the Middle Ages, when many people were illiterate, teaching took place through images or pictures. The Wheel of Life was an image so important that it was often carved in the stone walls of cathedrals for all to see. People viewing the image were receiving instructions about the nature of change. What were the lessons?

At the top of the Wheel of Life is a well-dressed, smiling, kingly or queenly person. This person is in the position of Happiness. Life is normal and things are going well. When change occurs, the wheel turns with a clockwise movement. The same person, now with a look of distress, is upside down and falling through space. This is the position of Loss. The wheel continues its movement, and at the bottom of the wheel the individual is now nude and is being pulled through the muck and mire of life. This is the position of Suffering. The wheel turns once more, and the individual, who is again clothed, rises up to the position of Hope. From Hope there is anticipation of returning to the state of Happiness. One lesson of the Wheel of Life is that these four positions or phases of happiness, loss, suffering, and hope are the only possibilities in life, and we are always in the midst of one of them or moving on to another.

Happy is where everything seems normal. Happy is where we all want to be. It is here that whatever we are doing is succeeding. Life is smooth, we have a routine that works, and we are comfortable.

Loss is where the routine of happiness begins to fall apart. A variety of events have signaled the coming of change, and we are challenged to let go of the routine that has worked. When loss comes, we want to return to happiness as quickly as possible. We want to regain our equilibrium by making the wheel go in reverse. The wheel, however, only moves clockwise. To regain happiness, we must follow the wheel into suffering.

Suffering is at the bottom of the wheel. Suffering is the process of transition. The Latin root word for suffering means "to experience" or "to allow." To suffer means that we must go through and fully experience our loss, so we can make, and then implement, plans for a return to normalcy. If we want to return to happiness, the process of suffering cannot be short-circuited. We cannot go over, under, or around this transition phase. We must go through it with the hard work of becoming conscious of our responsibility and choices. In the phase of suffering, we must devise a coping strategy for changing. The work of this process is often unpleasant because it brings the accompanying normal but distressing emotions of tension, anxiety, worry, frustration, anger, conflict, and sadness. It is out of the suffering and "living-through" experience that hope arises.

Hope comes only when our plan and our efforts at coping are working and progress is seen. We begin to feel competent. Our goal comes into view, and we have a vision of the return to the happiness of normality. The normality that we find, however, will not be the same as the "old normal." Through an effective process of change we return to balance, but it is a new and different balance. Happiness is found again, but in a new and different state of equilibrium.

Once back to normal, if we look ahead, the uneasy sense that change is coming again appears on the horizon. The winds of change are always blowing. The Wheel of Life always turns. Our happiness—our normality—is not a permanent state. More change will come, and the journey around the wheel into loss, suffering, and hope begins again. This is the normal life process of growth and development toward increasing levels of maturity.

Whenever change enters our life, we experience the emotions of change. As we sense that loss is coming there is anxiety, apprehension, and worry. When loss arrives we feel sad, angry, irritated, and frustrated. Grieving needs to be done. With the experience of the living through or suffering of change may come stress, depression, burnout, helplessness, or even hopelessness. Eventually, hope brings a renewal of energy, optimism, and enthusiasm, while a return to happiness brings a sense of satisfaction, accomplishment, and contentment.

The Wheel of Life teaches that we cannot get happy and stay happy. Change always occurs and brings with it the possibility of growth. The different phases and emotions of change are expected and normal. These phases cannot be avoided. Look for and accept them in yourself and others, and you will be better able to work through the recurrent process of change.

❖❖❖

- ◆ Where are you on the Wheel of Life today?
- ◆ Where were you yesterday? Has it already turned?
- ◆ Sometimes the Wheel turns fast, and sometimes slowly. Watch yourself today, and see what the Wheel does.
- ◆ What can you do to speed up or slow down the Wheel?

Lesson 52

The Search for Happiness

There are lots of ways of being miserable, but only one way of being comfortable, and that is to stop running round after happiness. If you make up your mind not to be happy there's no reason why you shouldn't have a fairly good time.

~ Edith Wharton

Ask most people what they want in life and the answer will be—happiness. Sometimes the answer is whined as in, "I just want to be happy. Is that too much too ask?" Well, … yes, it is. You see the problem in life is that you cannot get happy and stay happy. Happiness is temporary. It doesn't last.

While most of us know this is true, we don't accept it. We secretly hope to attain the happiness that will endure. We want to reach a plateau of happiness and stay there.

Maybe in high school you thought that if you could just graduate, life would be good, but after graduation, you needed a job. If you could only find a good one, you would be happy, but once you got a job, now you needed a promotion. Maybe if you got married, you would be happy? However, the honeymoon always wears off. Perhaps you thought, "If I just have kids, then I will be happy." Soon you were thinking, "If these kids ever leave home, that is when I will be happy." Maybe when you retire…? Maybe in the afterlife…? The problem is that happiness is ever receding.

Furthermore, if you did get happy and stay happy, you would not know it after two weeks. You would have reached a plateau where things are the same day after day, and the word for this is *bored*. After two weeks on a tropical, desert island you would realize, "There's is nothing to do here. I have already done it all." In life, we must have both ups and downs in order to be happy. The only way you can be happy today is for you to have been unhappy yesterday. You have to have a point of comparison in order to appreciate what you have. You can get happy. You just can't stay that way. If you are happy today, enjoy it because it *will* not last.

The best way to be happy is to fully live in the present moment. This way you appreciate what you have while you have it. Learn to live in the present moment, and you may find that it is happy no matter what is going on around you.

Most of us don't do this. Our minds are either in the past of remembered hurt, loss, and regret, or in the future of imagined fears and unrealized hopes. We are rarely in the present moment, which *is* the only moment we have, and *is* where happiness resides.

Once we accept that we can't get happy and stay happy, we may become happy. Look around your life today. Where were you yesterday? Maybe today is already better than you think. Maybe you are happy and don't know it. Wake up to the present moment. Enjoy what you have.

❖❖❖❖

- ◆ Recall a time when you robbed yourself of happiness by dwelling on the past.
- ◆ Recall a time when you robbed yourself of happiness by anticipating the future.
- ◆ Are you in the present moment now? Is it happy?
- ◆ What can you do to stay in the present moment as much as possible?

Lesson 53

Letting Go

Every exit is an entrance somewhere else.

~ Tom Stoppard

Change always begins with loss. The first step of change is letting go. If you are going to change, you will lose something because you can't stay the same and change at the same time. You must let go of where you are in order to get to where you are going. Such an act of letting go involves loss and the typical emotions of loss: sadness, anxiety, fear, irritation, frustration, and grief. Since most of us do not like these feelings, we try to avoid change and the necessary losses that accompany it.

Whether change is positive or negative and whether it is desired or not, loss is always involved. Suppose that you have been seeking a promotion at work. When it finally comes, you are given a huge salary increase and transferred to another state. While this is a good and exciting change, as you arrive at your new job, you realize that you lost some things along the way.

For example, having left family, friends, and co-workers, you are now lonely in your new location. You live in unfamiliar surroundings and can't find your way until you learn the city. You don't have a supportive church, synagogue, or mosque to attend. You no longer have your old comforting routine of daily life. Most importantly, you have lost a sense of competence in your job. You knew how to do the one you had, but you are now in a new position. It requires a higher level of skills and abilities, and you are as yet unproven. In this phase of adjustment, you may become momentarily homesick and wonder if you made the right decision.

When change is not desired but is thrust upon you, such as the loss of a job or a divorce, the experience of loss is more difficult. The disruption will be greater, and the emotions will be more intense than when you sought change. If the loss involves a death, you move into grief. All changes bring loss and require the work of letting go. Some changes just bring greater loss and need more work than others.

What is the work of letting go? At the simplest level, it is acknowledging the losses. It is thinking through a planned change and preparing for what is to come. You must be aware of a loss if you are to deal with it. Knowing what is coming is helpful.

With sudden change, however, you cannot plan and must remain open to the emotions that arise. Denial and looking the other way will not help. Locking feelings up inside only allows them to grow outside of awareness until they can no longer be contained, and many times they burst forth in explosions of emotion or the physical symptoms of stress. When going through a significant loss, certain steps are often found to be helpful.

- Talk to someone you trust. Share what you are going through. You will often find that your feelings are normal, and that others have been there before you. Their listening can help.
- Find a support group for your specific issue. There are many groups such as newcomers clubs, divorce recovery groups, and groups that focus specifically on grief.
- Take action. Directly confront the situation. Do what needs to be done. Get results and you will feel more in control.
- Be good to yourself. Don't neglect your needs. Reward yourself with small pleasures. Keep your spirits up.

Remember that change always begins with loss. Loss is normal and is part of the process of growth. Learn to embrace your losses, and see if you move through your changes more quickly.

❖❖❖❖

- Recall a recent positive change such as a move to a new home.
- Were there any regrets? Any second thoughts?
- Did you lose anything, perhaps a short commute to work?
- How did you become aware of the loss? What did you do?

Lesson 54

The Safe Emotion

*Anger will never disappear so long as thoughts of resentment
are cherished in the mind. Anger will disappear just as soon as
thoughts of resentment are forgotten.* ~ Buddha

Life has many normal emotional states which are stimulated by
varying circumstances. Happiness, sadness, anger, joy, fear,
embarrassment, and hurt are among these normal feelings. Of the
variety of emotions that we can feel and express, one is safer to
show than all the others. This emotion is safe because with it you
can predict what kind of response you will receive in return.

What is the safest, risk–free emotion? It is anger. Why is it
safe? It is safe because when you show anger, you expect to get
anger in return. Fuss at the sales clerk, and he/she may fuss back.
Criticize your spouse, and you can expect to get criticism. There is
no surprise. Anger is a boomerang that always returns. This is not
to say don't express your anger. Sometimes anger is the only correct and productive emotion to use. It is just that when anger is
shown, little risk is involved. You are only surprised if the response
you receive is not one of anger.

The problem with easily shown anger is that often it is not the
emotion truly being felt. Almost always the true emotions beneath
the anger are sadness and hurt. These emotions are not as safe to
show because it is less predictable what you will get in return.
Show your sadness, and you may get indifference. No one may
care. Show your hurt, and others may only laugh at your sensitivi-
ty. Your sadness and hurt may only increase.

An even deeper emotion can underlie sadness and hurt. It is
fear. Our loneliness, our sense of being lost, and our confusion
about what to do in a difficult situation frightens us. We don't want
to show our fear because it seems like weakness. If we are feeling

frightened, we hide it away and focus on the hurt, the loss, or the unfairness of it all. Anger springs forth, providing a momentary sense of power, and we lash out at those around us.

Anger, the safe emotion, distances us from others, blocks understanding, and increases alienation. If people *only* show anger, it is difficult to learn that beneath our anger, we are all vulnerable human beings. While I may know of my personal sense of hurt, sadness, and fear, you, on the other hand, seem to have no such concerns. If we lock away from each other our more painful but risky emotions, no ground for empathy exists. I think that I am the only one with these messy, uncomfortable feelings, and you think the same. If we are to understand one another, the barrier of easily expressed anger must come down.

Someone has to go first. Who will be brave enough to drop the anger? Whoever does is taking a risk. The response will be uncertain; however, it just might be one of real communication.

It could be a relief if someone told the truth about how they feel because now I can tell the truth as well. Once someone takes the first step, we no longer have to hide behind anger but can open our hearts to concern and understanding. Once we do so, life will begin to go better.

❖❖❖❖

- ◆ Recall a recent time when you were angry.
- ◆ Look beneath the anger. Can you find hurt or sadness?
- ◆ What might have happened had you shown these emotions?
- ◆ Look beneath the hurt and sadness.Can you can find fear?
- ◆ What was the fear about?
- ◆ What might have happened if you talked about the fear?

Lesson 55

Forgiveness Is for You

This is certain, that a man that studieth revenge keeps his wounds green, which otherwise would heal and do well.

~ Francis Bacon

The weak can never forgive. Forgiveness is the attribute of the strong. ~ Mahatma Gandhi

At one time or another we all have been hurt in our relationships. Some hurts are minor, such as personal slights, bruised feelings, or embarrassing moments. Other hurts are profound, as with acts of emotional or physical abuse. In either case, the reaction to the hurt is to sometimes say, "I will never forgive." Maybe you have made this statement. If you have, then consider this question: When you don't forgive, who suffers?

What happens when you don't forgive? Frequently you will think about the hurt. Events of the day remind you. You might see a person on the street and remember what he/she did to you. Someone mentions a name and the hurt is rekindled. A song on the radio stirs the embers of the pain. You might work with people who hurt you or even live with them. Every day you are be reminded of what happened.

Once reminded, you start thinking about how bad it was, how unfair it was, how you didn't deserve it, and about the terrible effect it had on your life. You are filled with anger and resentment or sadness and loss. You say once again, "I will never forgive." At this point who is feeling bad? Who is miserable? The answer is "You!"

What is the other person doing? Most likely, not busy thinking about you. He/she may not even remember what happened or know you were hurt. He/she may not care that you were hurt or may have an entirely different view of what took place. The other person is feeling fine. You are not, but you keep thinking about how bad it was. Your suffering grows.

Your lack of forgiveness is only hurting you. You end up in a state of misery by the end of the day. What would happen if you were to forgive? Who would get better? Again, the answer is "You."

You must remember—forgiveness is always for you. You don't forgive for the other person. You forgive so you can get better. Forgiveness is a letting go. It is a freeing of yourself.

The other person or people involved do not have to know that you have forgiven them. You don't necessarily call them up and tell them. You might not be able to tell them. Maybe you can't locate them, or they might be deceased. They never have to know that you have forgiven them. They might not care if they did know.

If it is true that forgiveness is for you, why is it so difficult? It is difficult because forgiving can seem like "giving in" or being weak. We don't want to be weak; so, we don't forgive. It can seem like an approval of what happened. We may worry that forgiving might be an invitation to be mistreated again. Not forgiving can also create a sense of power and control through holding a grudge. It seems to get revenge, especially if the person who hurt us actually wants to be forgiven. Moreover, we may fear that forgiving might lead to forgetting, and we don't want to forget and be open to any future hurts.

Not forgiving and holding onto a resentment is like having a wound which you check every day to see if it is healing. Each day you open it up to look, and sure enough, it is not any better. To heal from a wound, you must stop opening it every day. To heal from hurt, you must stop reliving it every day. You must learn to let go.

The reality is that forgiveness frees you. It recaptures the energy that you are giving away in bitterness, anger, hatred, and revenge. Forgiveness empowers you. It puts you back in charge of you.

Forgiveness can also rebuild relationships. This may be important. Holding a grudge can be a roadblock to progress. Others may want and seek your forgiveness. If so, forgiveness would help you and also them, but helping them is not essential to forgiveness.

Do you want to be bitter or better? This is the forgiveness choice. Hold on to the pain, and you will be bitter. Make the better choice. Learn to let go. Learn to be a forgiving person.

❖❖❖❖

- What is the longest that you have carried a grudge?
- Who suffered most because of your grudge?
- Do you hold any current resentments?
- Choose one and let it go. See if you can get your energy back.

Lesson 56

Midlife Crisis and the Search for Meaning

Midlife is when you reach the top of the ladder and find that it is against the wrong wall. ~ Joseph Campbell

Midlife is the old age of youth and the youth of old age.
~ Proverb

Seventy-six million "Baby Boomers" are facing midlife. While midlife is a time of change and transition, it is only a normal stage of life, like childhood or adolescence. Saying it is normal means that it cannot be avoided. Live long enough and you will encounter it. As you could not avoid adolescence, so you cannot avoid midlife. Midlife may be denied, but it cannot be escaped.

Midlife is greatly misunderstood. It is essentially a positive experience that has the goal of making you a whole person. It is trying to transform you from one level of living to another. Adolescence transformed you from a child into an adult. It may not have been a pleasant experience, but it was not meant to be fun. It was meant to change you. Midlife also intends to change you, and you may not enjoy it. Midlife is trying to guide you toward psychological and spiritual wholeness. At midlife you are only halfway to that goal. More growth is needed but may be resisted if you have become comfortably stuck where you are.

While midlife provides the opportunity to enliven life, many people think that it is a time to recapture lost youth. This is a common but a great misunderstanding. The challenge of midlife is not to become young again but to grow into your full potential. The midlife experience provides an opening to psychological and spiritual growth that allows and empowers a giving back to others and the community. Midlife is a time to give up your self-centered nature and to nurture others.

In life, we have two major identity crises. The first, occurring in adolescence, is to establish an identity. You must develop a sense of who you are. You focus on achievement and accomplishment. You acquire a unique personality style. You become "you," but the danger is that "you" may be overly focused on yourself. The second identity crisis is at midlife when you must give up who you think you are, so you can become who you were meant to be. This transitional requirement of letting go is not easy and is greatly resisted, invariably leading to the well-known "midlife crisis."

Ultimately, midlife is about the search for true meaning in life. Whenever we ask about meaning, we have asked a spiritual question. Midlife is an opportunity for an awakening into a deeper spirituality. A deepening spirituality always takes us into caring for and giving to others. Midlife is trying to make us loving people who can focus less on ourselves and more on others, but this is a difficult change, and the midlife journey cannot be taken without a certain amount of suffering.

To suffer means to live through or to allow an experience into your life. At midlife you must suffer—live through—the loss, change, and letting go of much of what you bring into it. You must give up one identity for another. It is rather like the transformation from a caterpillar into a butterfly in that it is neither pleasant nor guaranteed, but if you don't take the journey, you stagnate.

Midlife wants to take you on a journey of transformation. It wants to make you a more loving person. Are you willing to take the journey? Are you willing to let go of who you are in order to see who you can become?

❖❖❖❖

- ◆ Have you become increasingly dissatisfied with who you are?
- ◆ What is the nature of the dissatisfaction?
- ◆ Does it seem that something is missing from your life?
- ◆ What is it that you want?
- ◆ Are you on a quest for meaning?

Lesson 57

Mind Storms

Be thou the rainbow to the storms of life, The evening beam that smiles the clouds away, And tints tomorrow with prophetic ray!
~ Lord Byron

Meditation teacher Sylvia Boorstein has written a simple but profound book on Buddhist spirituality with the intriguing title of *It's Easier than You Think.* In it she talks about the Buddhist concept of Mind Hindrances. These are the five energies that traditional Buddhism identifies as impediments to the clear seeing of life events.

The five energies are lust, aversion, torpor, restlessness, and doubt. We often talk of them as neediness, anger, low energy, fear, and demoralization. As occasionally encountered experiences, they can make life problematic, but these occasional and normal hindrances can intensify into something more lasting. If they do so, they may change from Mind Hindrances into Mind States.

A Mind State is a Hindrance that is not transient. It comes to stay. A Mind State becomes a habitual outlook and routine response pattern. All life experiences are filtered through the Mind State. The Mind State of Lust looks at everything through the lens of neediness and desire. Something is missing, and life is not satisfactory. The Angry Mind State is always on the verge of irritation and frustration and fills the air with tension. Habitual Lethargy as a Mind State robs life of the energy required for day to day tasks and leaves none left over for new adventures. The Fearful Mind State spreads anxiety into all areas of life while the Mind State of Doubt creates an insecure world of low self-esteem.

Mind States are difficult to live with because they make life more fretful or tedious than needed. They become the lenses though which life is viewed. A Mind State is hard to recognize and harder still to give up. It just seems to be the reality.

The true danger of Mind States, however, is that they can suddenly swirl up into Mind Storms. A Mind Storm is a Mind State out of control. Mind Storms blow in due to some real or imagined occurrence and can reek havoc while present. In a Mind Storm, comments are made and actions are taken that are later regretted. With a Mind Storm in control, clear vision is lost, and judgment is clouded. Just as the storms of weather come and go, so do the storms of the Mind. They blow in, and they blow out again, and then the damage must be surveyed.

Mind Storms always give warning signs. They initially show up in that small Voice of Conscience that talks to us. You might recognize it as that positive Voice saying, "Gee, you look good." And, "That was a terrific job." Or, in its negative tones, when it says, "That was really stupid. How could you be so dumb?"

In a Mind Storm, the Voice is usually negative, critical, or irrational in its comments. It is important to become aware of the Voice of Conscience while not responding too seriously to its comments. Our Voice of self-talk can talk us into some bad spots. The challenge of confronting Mind Storms is to learn to watch them come and go but not to react by feeding them more energy through an escalation of negative thinking and impulsive deeds.

❖❖❖❖

- ◆ Do you know your Mind Hindrances?
- ◆ Do you have a favorite one?
- ◆ What are your "weather signs" for an impending Storm?
- ◆ Can you catch yourself talking yourself into a Mind Storm?
- ◆ Watch your "weather" today and see what you notice.

Lesson 58

Anatomy of a Mind Storm: Part One

Worry is a futile thing, it's somewhat like a rocking chair,
although it keeps you occupied, it doesn't get you anywhere.

~ Anonymous

Being aware of the importance of attitude on daily life and knowing about Mind Hindrances and Mind States provides no guarantee of protection from Mind Storms. Given the right conditions, a Mind Storm thunders in and takes over before you know it. Once present, it is difficult to recognize.

Here is an example of one of my memorable Mind Storms. It had been brewing for a week and arrived with full force on a Friday evening.

My wife and I had been invited by friends to visit their beach house for the weekend. It was about a 300-mile, six-hour trip. We were to arrive several hours before our friends, pick up a key for the condo, and wait for them to arrive. Having never been to this location before, I felt some hesitancy about these plans. Nonetheless, I agreed to go.

The week leading up to the trip was very busy. In addition to working every day, I was out three evenings at meetings or classes. Tuesday and Thursday nights I was taking a computer class that met from 6:00 to 10:00 p.m. Wednesday night I was at a Church Education meeting. All day Thursday I was away from the office at a workshop and then went straight to the computer class. Arriving home that night, I realized that I had been in classes from 9:00 a.m. until 10:00 p.m. I was feeling resentful of such a busy schedule, even though it was self-chosen. My Voice of Conscience was saying, *You never have anytime for yourself. You never get to do what you want. You always have a meeting of some sort.*

The next day, Friday, I was scheduled to be off work but had been asked to come in and teach a special class at 7:00 a.m. Upon arrival, I learned that several staff members had called in sick, and the class was cancelled. I could have stayed home. The Little Voice spoke up. *This is stupid. Nobody respects your time. Nobody cares if you are inconvenienced. Your classes are always getting cancelled.*

I had been offering monthly classes at a counseling center. On Wednesday morning, I was interviewed on the local morning television news to announce the latest class. While still at work on Friday morning, I telephoned the center to ask how many people had called to sign up. I was told none, and the class was being cancelled. Again I heard, *Why do you even bother? Obviously, no one wants to hear what you have to say. You have been trying for a year with no success. Why don't you just quit? It's hopeless.*

On this same morning I was also having a tightness in the chest. I thought, *Maybe something is wrong. Your recent checkup was okay, but who knows? What if you get ill while away?*

Leaving the office after learning of the cancelled classes, I remembered that because of the busyness of the previous day, I had not had time to pack. Driving home I heard, *You always pack in advance. Now you are going to rush. You will forget something you need. Why does everything always happen to you? You never have enough time.*

Arriving home, I found that the stray dog that has been hanging around the neighborhood was at my house with my two dogs. *Great! This dog is probably sick and will make my dogs sick just like what happened to my cat. I need to stay home, catch that dog, and take it away. I need to be home to protect my dogs. I'll come back and find them sick. Why does something like this always happen when I am going out of town?*

I chased away the dog, quickly packed, and with my Voice of Conscience still babbling in the background, left for the beach around noon. It was a very pretty day. The sky was blue, and the weather was nice. The drive to the coast was pleasant.

❖❖❖❖

- Do you have a voice carrying on a running dialogue like this?
- What do you hear from your voice?
- Can you catch it in action?
- Can you turn it off?

Lesson 59

Anatomy of a Mind Storm: Part Two

You don't need a weatherman to know which way the wind blows.

~ Bob Dylan

U pon arriving at our friend's condo at the private resort, we drove to the guardhouse at the main entrance. There had been an auto accident on the grounds and the guard was gone. A young woman from the reception desk had been called into duty, and she was very stressed. She knew nothing about the key we were to pick up and could find no evidence of it. I went to the property management office and found a woman who did know we were coming. She called the guardhouse with the correct key number. (Our friends had inadvertently given us the wrong address.) I returned to the guardhouse and found that the young woman was still frantic, but with some effort she was able to find the key.

When we finally arrived at the condo, the key would not fit. It did not go all the way into the lock. Nothing I could do would open the lock. I drove back to the guardhouse only to find that a rather large, stern, female guard had returned. She was initially somewhat suspicious about why I had a key at all and about how I got it. As I explained, she became more cooperative and said she would come and check the lock. The guard seemed to assume that I just did not know what to do. She soon followed me back to the condo but could not get the key to fit. She decided that something was broken off in the lock. She left saying she would call maintenance to come and check it.

A short while later the maintenance person arrived. He was friendly and talkative as he worked for about thirty minutes to remove the obstacle from the lock. He left to go to his workshop for a needed tool and returned telling me that we had been given the wrong key, and that nothing was caught in the lock. He also had determined that the condo was private property and not one of the resort's rentals. He had no other keys and could not make one. He would not help further because he would be "breaking and entering." He did take me to see the resort manager where it was agreed there was nothing they could do because the condo was private property.

It was now about six o'clock in the evening. My wife and I had been trying to get into the condo for two hours. We decided to go eat dinner and just wait.

We chose a highly recommended restaurant and planned to have a long, leisurely meal, but the restaurant was dark and unpleasant. It had a fast food atmosphere. There were a series of misadventures (misinformation, mixed up orders, wrong food). It was not a very pleasant place to wait.

We left, deciding to ride around and find some other place to pass the time. Maybe we could go shopping or catch a movie? It was close to 7:00 p.m. This was in February. It was chilly. Clouds had moved in. Every place we found was either closing or closed. No theaters were around. There seemed to be no convenient place to wait. We drove back to the condo to see if perhaps our friends had arrived early. They had not.

It was now five hours after our arrival. As I sat in the car in the cold and the dark, the Mind Storm that had been brewing showed up. *All the plans you make always go wrong. This is a bad omen. The weekend cannot go well. You should have stayed home. Whenever you go away things go wrong. It is not worth all the trouble. You should never leave home again. Your friends may not have another key. The lock may, in fact, be broken. You will have to sit in the car another three or four hours. You could be back home in that same amount of time. You should leave!*

Now, what would be a reasonable thing to do in this situation? It would make sense to find a place to wait. Any place would do. A motel lobby would be fine. We could explain our situation and just read while waiting.

Well, the Voice of Conscience kept talking to me, and it had even more to say. After a while I turned to my wife and blurted out something like, "Everything always happens to us. We are going home." No objection was heard. Mind States can be contagious.

So, we left and drove home. It took another five hours to reach our house. We arrived after midnight and crashed into bed.

❖❖❖

- ◆ Can you recall any recent Mind Storms of your own?
- ◆ Write out your Storm and analyze it to see what happened.
- ◆ How long had the Storm been building?
- ◆ What were the signs that it was coming?
- ◆ How could you have avoided it?

Lesson 60

Mind Storm Aftermath

Each of us makes his own weather, determines the color of the skies in the emotional universe which he inhabits.

~Fulton J. Sheen

Waking up on Saturday morning, a new Mind Storm set in. *What have you done? How could you have been so stupid? All you had to do was wait. What was wrong with you?*

As this new Mind Storm continued in the background, I called and apologized to my friends. They had arrived with a key and had no trouble getting in. Having read the hastily written, somewhat cryptic note I left, they were wondering what had happened.

The new Storm of self-blame continued most of Saturday. On Sunday I went to a class at church where we were studying Boorstein's book. As I confessed my lapse from the Buddhist ideal of the Peaceful Mind, the Storm lessened.

Mind States come and go. Sometimes a Mind State turns into a Storm. The challenge of mindfulness is to catch the Storm early and stop it. If you can't stop it, just let it blow itself out. Don't get caught up in it and don't act it out.

I regret to say that I was swept away by a Storm that had been brewing for a week. What I thought was a decision made from the frustration of the moment, was actually made from the frustration of the day and the week. I allowed myself to slip into a Mind Storm and did not realize it until the Storm passed. I thought it was about one thing (the key that didn't fit), when it was about many things. The lesson of the moment was to learn patience, but I thought it had to do with bad decisions and bad luck. I missed the lesson of patience that I was offered because I left and returned home.

Mind Storms are hard to recognize when they are present. They seem to be the reality. In reality, they are the illusion. So, watch the horizon of your mind. Look for the warning signs of a change in the weather. If Storms do appear, just let them pass. Remember: The weather always changes.

❖❖❖❖

- How do you know if your "weather" is about to change?
- What helps you to let a Mind Storm pass?

Lesson 61

Positive Quitting

It is a good answer that knows when to stop.

~ Italian Proverb

If you aspire to the highest place, it is no disgrace to stop at the second, or even the third. ~ Cicero

A re you a quitter? Do you know when to stop? Or, do you sometimes continue something much too long. In life it helps to know when to quit. It helps to know when to give up.

Quitting can be difficult because we have certain beliefs about quitters. There is the old saying, "A winner never quits, and a quitter never wins." This is true about some things in life. Persistence is often needed to reach a goal. Failure frequently comes before success. If you quit after a failure, you may rob yourself of eventual victory. A proverb for success says, "Fall down eight times but get up nine." The ninth try may be the winner. Don't give up too easily.

A problem with quitting, however, is that not knowing when to quit can also block success. Sometimes you must quit something in order to succeed. For example, you could:

- Quit procrastinating. Get to work on what needs to be done.
- Quit stressing out over the small hassles of life and relax.
- Quit being so irritable.
- Quit being so hard to please.
- Quit expecting perfection from yourself or others.
- Quit trying to control everything.
- Quit trying to do it all yourself.
- Quit hanging out with negative people.
- Quit doing what doesn't work.

- Quit doing the same thing but expecting a different result.
- Quit working all the time and have some fun.
- Quit activities that do not bring meaning into your life.

What are some things that you need to quit? What could you stop doing that would make your life better? See if you can identify, and then *stop,* doing those things in life that are harmful to you. Learn to make better choices. Quit your bad habits and develop some good ones.

When you do quit something, make sure you have a plan for what you will begin. Don't just leave an empty space in your life. It may soon be filled by another bad habit. If you choose to stop stressing-out, what will you do to relax? If you are going to be less irritable, how will you practice calmness? If you give up caffeine, what will take its place? Remember: When you quit a bad habit, develop a good one.

In life, quitting something often helps, so consider becoming a quitter. Become a positive quitter. Practice positive quitting. Stop those things that you know you don't need to be doing, and see if your life begins to go better.

❖❖❖❖

- How do you feel about quitting?
- Have you ever quit something?
- How did you react?
- How did others react?
- Has your life ever been improved by quitting something?
- What bad habits could you quit?

Lesson 62

Living Life Inside Out

The worst is not so long as we can say, "This is the worst."
~ William Shakespeare

Peace of mind is that mental condition in which you have accepted the worst.   ~ Lin Yutang

Life is lived from the inside out. Our experience of life is based not only on what happens to us but also on what we believe about what happens. It is our belief that actually determines our reaction and creates our experience. Our belief resides inside of us in our thinking. What we believe acts like a lens through which we see the world, and our beliefs color what we see. Positive beliefs brighten our life; negative, pessimistic beliefs darken it. We live life from the inside out. We live it through our beliefs.

Eric Butterworth, a well-known Unity minister, says, "Things may happen to you, things may happen around you, but the only things that really count are the things that happen in you." The things happening in you are your thoughts and your understandings about the things happening to and around you.

Once we accept this simple fact, we are placed in charge of our lives. While we cannot control what happens to and around us, we can control our thinking. We can learn to listen to how we talk to ourselves and discover when we are talking nonsense and creating more misery than we need.

Sometimes in our inner dialogue, we tend to exaggerate. Something happens that we don't like, and we start "awfulizing." We say things like, "This is terrible." Or, "I can't stand it." Or, "This is the worst thing that can happen. I might as well just give up." We create a negative expectation that can become a self-ful-filling prophecy. To make life go better, we must learn to challenge our thinking and ensure that we are realistic in our assessment of the events of life. Things may be tough enough without our awfulizing about them.

Here is a simple way to stop the awfulizing. The next time you hear yourself saying that something is the "worst," call a time-out. Now, imagine one or two things that could have happened but did not, and how they would have made your situation even worse than it is. You can always do this. You see, the situation is not as bad as it could be, and you can give thanks for what didn't happen. Your outlook and experience will improve. You may still be in a tough spot, but you are not making it worse by adding to it.

Learn to live life from the inside out. Always check out your beliefs and stop the awfulizing. Live from your realistic but positive beliefs, and see if life begins to go better.

❖❖❖❖

- Listen for your "awfulizing" voice today.
- How do you make things awful for yourself?
- What do you typically say?
- Catch yourself in action and stop the process.

Lesson 63

The Spiritual Practice of Elevator Courtesy

Three things in human life are important: The first is to be
kind. The second is to be kind. And the third is to be kind.

~ Henry James

Have you ever impatiently waited for an elevator as you pushed the call button again and again? Rushing on, when it finally arrives, you bump into passengers as they are trying to get off, and then you turn and stand passively watching as the door slams shut in someone's face. Next, standing in shoulder-to-shoulder silence, facing the door, and preparing to jump out, you frustratingly count off the floors as you pause at each and every one on the way to your stop.

You have just had an opportunity for a spiritual practice—for the practice of elevator courtesy. A spiritual practice is an activity we do with the intention of gaining self-understanding and also connecting ourselves to others in creative relationships. Spiritual practices come in many forms, such as prayer, meditation, and reading scripture. Joseph Campbell, the mythologist, said that his practice was "underlining sentences"—the daily work of study. A spiritual practice is something that enlivens your life and also chal-lenges it. It challenges you to be different; it challenges you to change.

Riding the elevator can be a spiritual practice because it offers to teach patience, kindness, tolerance, self-sacrifice, forgiveness, and the surrender of control.

The next time you wait for an elevator, see if you can practice patience. Press the call button once and wait. Once summoned, the elevator comes, but in its own good time. It comes no faster with frantic effort, which only gives you the illusion of control. Surrender the illusion and while patiently waiting, enjoy the peaceful moment that life has offered you. Be observant and look around. Who are your fellow travelers? Do they need assistance? Could you be of help when the elevator arrives? Perhaps you could hold the door or carry a package.

When the door does open, make sure you let all the passengers out before you rush on. In fact, don't rush on. Practice kindness. Let others go first. If the elevator fills up, take the next one. Practice peaceful waiting. When you enter the elevator, mindfully notice if others are rushing to catch it and then hold the door for them.

Once aboard, challenge yourself to break the elevator code of "eyes-forward silence." As you move to the back, making room for others, speak to your neighbors with a friendly greeting such as "Good morning" or "Nice day." Take a chance. Make eye contact. Smile.

Practice forgiveness when someone holds the door a little too long or when the next entering passenger accidentally leans against the control panel causing unnecessary stops at every floor. When you do reach your floor, gracefully let others exit ahead of you before proceeding toward your destination.

Each time you approach an elevator, remember the practice of elevator courtesy. Center yourself with the intention of being mindful. Observe yourself and your reactions. If you wander away from the ideal of elevator courtesy, just return to the effort. You may find that riding the elevator transforms your life. Ride the elevator enough, and you may become a kinder and more loving person.

❖❖❖❖

- ◆ Recall your most recent elevator experience.
- ◆ Did you practice patience and kindness?
- ◆ The next time you ride an elevator, intentionally hold the door for someone.
- ◆ Be sure you press the call button just once.

Lesson 64

Attitudes of Gratitude

Joy is the simplest form of gratitude.

~ Karl Barth

Sometimes you hear it said of a person that they have an *attitude*. This usually means a *bad* attitude, which is not only bad for them, but bad for you as well. However, not all attitudes are negative. They come in a variety of types. Attitudes are like opinions; everybody has one, and in life, attitudes are important.

What kind of attitude do you have? Is it good or bad? If you have a bad attitude, there is a simple way to improve it. Practice gratitude. Develop the attitude of gratitude. Learn to be grateful for what you have. Appreciate all the things in your life that make it worthwhile. You probably have more to appreciate than you know.

The easiest way to develop an attitude of gratitude is to keep a small notepad by your bedside. Each night as you get into bed, take a few moments to write out five things that happened during the day for which you are grateful. Review your day and look for the moments of gratitude. They may not be momentous. They can be very simple and ordinary. You may recall things such as:

◆ Your dog and his excitement at seeing you.
◆ A friend's hug and a child's smile.
◆ A stranger's kindness in the crowded check-out line.
◆ The rainbow you saw after the rain. Or, even, the rain itself.

Other items for gratitude may be more profound.

◆ A recovery from illness.
◆ The mending of a relationship.
◆ The birth of a grandchild.

Each day, practice being grateful for what you have. Be grateful for what comes your way. Intentionally look for the positive in your life, and write it down to claim it for yourself. Whenever you need to make a bad day go better, you can return to your Gratitude List and review it. You will be reminded of how much you already have, and then you can be grateful for your list as well.

If you work at developing an attitude of gratitude, you may transform yourself into a person for whom others are grateful. Your presence will begin to bring joy into the lives of others through your positive outlook and your appreciation for life. People will say of you that you have an attitude, and they will mean a *good* one.

Attitudes of gratitude are contagious. Be sure that you have yours well developed, so you can spread it everywhere you go.

❖❖❖❖

◆ What are you already grateful for today?
◆ What can you do to make another person grateful for you?
◆ Can you do it now?

Lesson 65

Circling to the Center

We shall not cease from exploration
And the end of all of our exploring
Will be to arrive where we started
And know the place for the first time.

~ T. S. Eliot

It has been said that life is like a maze. We do live in maze-like cities, work in huge, maze-like offices, and get caught in maze-like traffic jams. In life, we struggle to avoid blind alleys as we try to find the right path. We want the one that will take us straight to the goal we seek in the quickest and most direct way. Sometimes, however, we become lost and frightened, and we may *feel* like rats running a maze.

A maze is not the best image for life. It presents life as a problem to be solved and not an experience to be enjoyed. A similar but better image for life is that of a labyrinth. While it may look like a maze, it is not. A labyrinth has no dead ends. Only one path exists, and it always leads to the goal. You can't get lost even though sometimes you may feel that way.

A labyrinth is an ancient symbol which appears in all cultures; it serves as a metaphor for life's journey. It represents a pilgrimage to wholeness. A labyrinth can be seen as a journey to the deep center of ourselves where we seek understanding and healing. The labyrinth journey can help mend the brokenness of life. Traveling to the center, we find meaningful insights that can be brought out into the world to revitalize life.

Choose to enter a labyrinth and the path appears to take you straight to the center, but soon you take a detour. As you continue, each successive turn appears to take you further and further from the goal. You may start to feel lost and off track as if going in the wrong direction, but remember, on a labyrinth, you cannot get lost. Even if it feels unpleasant and confusing at the moment, you are always right where you need to be. Perseverance is required. Don't stop or turn back.

Keep following the path, and you will gain another glimpse of the goal, but again the path turns. Continuing, you are led away from the center and then closer and then away until, unexpectedly and with a surprise, you arrive at the destination you were seeking.

The simplest meaning of the labyrinth journey is that life never takes you straight to your goal. Life's journey always has ups and downs, highs and lows, and frequent times of feeling lost, but the "Labyrinth of Life" is always teaching you what you need to learn—if you can mindfully pay attention.

On a labyrinth, the center is only the halfway point. The labyrinth journey is one of seeking self-knowledge and under-standing, which must come out into the world where it can be given away to others in a creative relationship. The labyrinth experience opens us to ourselves and to others. When walked with a group, the labyrinth teaches us about the unity hidden in apparent diversity. There *is* only *one* path in life, and all are on it. We must learn to cooperate as we make the journey together.

❖❖❖❖

- The labyrinth and its lessons are best experienced by actually walking one.
- Try to find and visit a labyrinth near you.
- Spend some time in quiet reflection.
- Become centered and balanced.
- See what the labyrinth can teach you about your life's journey.

Lesson 66

The Labyrinth Map

I have an existential map. It has 'You are here' written all over it.
~ Steven Wright

Recently, I had the opportunity of introducing a group of 20 children, ages six to eleven, to the labyrinth. They were attending a Bible school class at a church which has an outdoor, seven-circuit labyrinth designed of stone. We talked together about mazes and labyrinths and to illustrate the difference, I gave the children several simple mazes to trace, and they all experienced getting lost by making a wrong turn. Next, I offered them an easy, three-circuit labyrinth and had them trace it. No one got lost. I asked about the difference between a maze and a labyrinth, and they easily recognized that you couldn't get lost in a labyrinth. There are no wrong turns.

For more of a challenge, I gave the children a large drawing of a seven-circuit labyrinth to trace with their fingers. As they were following the path, several children inadvertently crossed over the lines and became confused. We talked about how you had to pay close attention when tracing the finger labyrinth, but I assured them that when we went out to walk their labyrinth, none would get lost if they just stayed on the path. One young boy, about eight years old, held up his paper labyrinth and asked if he could take the Labyrinth Map with him. I hastily said, "No. Just leave it here. You don't need a map."

Once outside, I told the children that they could walk a labyrinth any way they wanted, but that for *today* we would walk it slowly and quietly. I had several parents with me who were helping to monitor the children. I decided to walk first, so I could model "slow and quiet" walking. The children were to follow me, and then the parents would walk.

Now, I have never actually observed children walking a labyrinth slowly and quietly because the labyrinth has its own energy that calls to children and asks them to run and shout. All went well for a few moments of slow walking, but as more and more children entered the labyrinth, the energy of it caught them. The noise level went up. There was running and stumbling, laughing and shouting, and "high fives" were being passed all along the path. Parents, both those already walking and those waiting to enter, were loudly whispering to the kids to slow down and be quiet. They made a valiant effort at control but to no avail. The joy of the labyrinth was contagious. A few parents even smiled and walked faster.

Several children who had run through the labyrinth wanted to do it again. One was the young boy with the Labyrinth Map. Secretly, he had put it into his pocket and was now taking it out for comparison. Back he went into the labyrinth with his map. He was carefully comparing his position in the labyrinth to the map, so he could tell where to go next. At each turn he evaluated where he was and how much progress he had made. He looked at his map to see where to go next. He would occasionally seem lost, but with the aid of his Labyrinth Map he made the journey to the center and back out again. He seemed quite pleased with his success.

I watched this young boy with amusement as he struggled to find the path he was already on with the aid of a map he didn't need. Suddenly, I realized what a wonderful image! What a metaphor! This is what we all do! We try to solve the Labyrinth of Life. We seek the experience of life in our minds through our thinking. We want to understand the journey in advance. We want to be prepared and avoid surprises. We want the security of a map. We want the map of intellectual concepts with the left-brain, logical, sequential, analytical assurance that we are going in the right direction.

In reality, the right or correct direction is always right before us if we will just give up the distraction of the map. If we move from left-brain to right-brain, open our eyes and drop the illusion of the map, we can clearly see the path and recognize that we are already on it. It *was* there all the time. It *is* there all the time. The path is one of intuition and faith. It always involves risk. This path is full of creativity and surprise and always takes us off the beaten path, the familiar path, toward where no map can go and where no map is of use. Each path in life is unique. My path is not yours; yours is not mine. We must each find our own way.

No Labyrinth Map exists, nor is one needed. This lesson is extraordinarily difficult to learn. We already have what we need. We are where we are supposed to be. *This* is *it,* if we give up the illusion that *it* is not. The map is not the territory. It never was. The map is not the experience. The map only points us toward it. Excessively relied upon, the map always takes us away from the experience.

We are all like the young boy with the Labyrinth Map. We all have our strategies and plans and our schematic diagrams of where life either *is* or *should* be going. While clinging to the Labyrinth Map robs us of the lived labyrinth experience, such clinging may also be necessary in order to lead us to the precipice where the trail disappears, and we are thrust onto our own resources. We may need the safety of a map until we eventually learn to trust our experience and ourselves.

Such trust may begin at the entrance to one of Life's Labyrinths, often disguised as one of life's crises, where we are forced to discard the Labyrinth Map and step into the journey to our own deep selves through a leap of faith.

Joseph Campbell sums up this journey to faith with a story: "A bit of advice given to a young Native American at the time of his initiation: 'As you go the way of life, you will see a great chasm. Jump. It is not as wide as you think.'"

❖❖❖❖

- ◆ Do you have a Labyrinth Map? Do you have a plan or expectation for the way life should be?
- ◆ Has your plan ever robbed you of a valuable life experience?
- ◆ Has it held you back?
- ◆ Has it limited your choices?
- ◆ Can you accept the challenge to put the aside your Labyrinth Map and take a risk?
- ◆ What would that risk be?

Lesson 67

Love and Marriage

Love is not altogether a delirium, yet it has many points in common therewith.

~ Thomas Carlyle

Being in love has been described as living in a temporary state of insanity. Falling in love, we lose our reason and act from unconscious motivation. When we fall in love, it is with our own idea of the perfect mate. In a sense, we always fall in love with ourselves because we carry in our mind's eye a picture of what the perfect companion will be like. This perfect image is created from years of imagination based upon magazines, movies, and mass media advertising. We know what we are looking for, and we search until we find it. We try to find someone who matches our ideal.

This matching process takes place through the psychological process of projection. Projection occurs when we meet a person who has a few of the characteristics we seek, so we assume that they have all of the qualities. We find a feature of the person that serves as a hook on which to hang our imagined image, and then we act as if the person *is* the ideal of our fantasy. We fall in love and into romantic obsession. Our sweethearts seems perfect and can do no wrong. They always have the right words or gestures, as well as delightful and intriguing habits that enliven our lives. We feel so lucky to have found our "one and only" that we want to be with them forever.

This state of adoration, this emotional high of intimacy, this state of obsession and temporary insanity has one guaranteed cure. Marriage.

Enter into marriage and the projection is bound to fail. Live with a person day in and day out and a few faults begin to show.

Some things about your partner you did not notice while in your "possessed" state. You overlooked that they are never on time, or can't seem to pick up clothes from the floor, or always squeeze the toothpaste tube from the wrong end. And that cute little laugh of theirs is slowly driving you to distraction. Your mate is falling short of your ideal, and you are falling out of love.

In disillusionment, many people want out of the relationship so they can get on with the search for their true love. This will never work because you always fall in love with your ideal, with the projection that you make, and this projection will always fail. No perfect people exist. In reality, once you are *dis–illusioned*, it is good news. It means that you see your mate without illusion. You see the person and the truth as it is, and you can learn to love the truth.

Once the illusion of romantic love is gone, the daily, hard work of real love, true love, can begin. In real love we accept each other as we are, faults and all, and we practice forgiveness of the small things (and maybe a few big things) with the hope that we, too, will be forgiven for falling short of our mate's ideal for us. If two people can do this, love can endure, and romance will blossom once again.

Remember to fall out of love as quickly as you can so you can get on with the work of building the true love relationship you want.

❖❖❖❖

- ◆ Can you identify your image of the ideal mate?
- ◆ Make a list of the desired qualities.
- ◆ Where did this image come from?
- ◆ How realistic is it?
- ◆ Have you been dis-illusioned before?
- ◆ Did you leave or stay?
- ◆ Are you up to the hard work of true love?

Lesson 68

The Ordeal of Marriage

A marriage without conflicts is almost as inconceivable as a nation without crises.

~ Andre Maurois

When two people are under the influence of the most violent, most insane, most delusive, and most transient of passions, they are required to swear that they will remain in that excited, abnormal, and exhausting condition continuously until death do them part.

~ George Bernard Shaw

The intensity of romantic love with its high flights of emotion and desire leads us to enter marriage, but then it always fades with the day to day work of maintaining the relationship. Many people do not understand this fact. They expect the emotional intensity of being in love to always be present, and when it is not, divorce is often considered. The realization is needed that marriage is actually hard work, and it is meant to be so.

Scott Peck has said that there are only two legitimate reasons for getting married. One reason is to have and raise children in a supportive environment, and the other reason is for the "friction" that marriage will bring into your life. This friction of the marriage relationship challenges you to grow and develop. The friction polishes you and removes the rough edges from your personality. The friction of marriage teaches you kindness, gentleness, and empathy for another that can become empathy for others.

John Sanford, author and Episcopal priest, has written that marriage is not for your happiness, but it is for your salvation. It is to save you from yourself and your self-centered nature, as it heals and makes you a whole person who can deeply love and care for another.

Joseph Campbell says of marriage that it is an "ordeal." He uses "ordeal" in the original sense of the word as a trial of experience that is meant to change you. Initiation rites always contain an ordeal, such as a vision quest, which must be endured as a transition from one state of being to another. Marriage is such an ordeal. It is a crucible of change that can awaken you to the possibility of transformation from a person who wonders what you can get for yourself into someone wondering what you can do for others.

If the essence of marriage—a journey that enables your growth and maturity—is not understood, when conflicts arise, the temptation is to end the marriage. While divorce will avoid the pain and challenge of the growth that marriage stimulates, at the same time it forces the process of personal development to grind to a halt. What's more, the problems that you do not work out in your first marriage will resurface in your second marriage, or the third, or fourth. Eventually, you have to face these conflicts because they are yours. You take them wherever you go. You cannot run away from them, and sooner or later they must be confronted if you are to learn to be a more mature person.

The ordeal of marriage offers us the possibility of facing what we must so we can learn what we need in order to become the people we are meant to be. Learning to engage the difficult but creative work of a marriage relationship provides an opportunity to lead a more meaningful life.

❖❖❖❖

- ◆ Have you lived through the difficult times in a committed relationship?
- ◆ What did you learn about yourself?
- ◆ How were you changed?
- ◆ How have you been polished by the friction of living together with another person?

Lesson 69

Four Levels of Healing

Just as your car runs more smoothly and requires less energy to go faster and farther when the wheels are in perfect alignment, you perform better when your thoughts, feelings, emotions, goals, and values are in balance.

~ Brian Tracy

Sometimes life falls apart, and we must put it back together again. When life is broken, we want to be made well again. We often seek a cure. To be cured is to eradicate a problem so that it no longer exists. Sometimes we can be cured of our problems, and sometimes we cannot. If we can't be cured, perhaps we can be healed.

Curing and healing are different. Healing is to be made whole, and it is fundamentally a psychological and spiritual process. Healing occurs when we accept the reality of what is and continue to live a full life anyway. Some people live through terrible ordeals and claim that their life was changed for the better because they learned how to become more open and loving. They made fundamental changes in their personality and lifestyle and moved toward wholeness.

Healing occurs at four levels. There is the level of the body, and this is what we usually focus on. We seek to make the body well and to be physically healthy. The other three levels of healing are the emotional, mental, and spiritual levels.

On the emotional level, healing is to be able to accept all of our emotions without judgment and to express them properly to others. It is not to lock them up inside and let them fester. It is not to have emotional explosions. It is not holding back from showing tenderness and love. Emotional healing is being aware of what you feel and being able to engage the emotion. Emotional healing lets us live fully and deeply.

The mental level refers to our thinking. It is about our attitudes, beliefs, and values. Mental healing comes with having the proper perspective on what you are experiencing. It is to understand clearly what is happening and to face it with a positive, realistic attitude. It is to avoid confusion and elaborate worrisome fantasies of what might go wrong. Mental healing keeps you focused in the moment and provides the wisdom needed for daily living.

Spiritual healing brings a deep sense of meaning and purpose. It provides a sense of connection to all that is. It centers you with that which is greater than you—a "higher power." You are able to look with awe on the simplest events of life and to appreciate the beauty of the smallest moment. No longer feeling isolated, you look at the world through the eyes of love and ask, "What can I do for others?"

Engage the four levels of healing every day and you will be taking steps toward your own healing.

- What are you doing today for your physical health?
- How are you opening to and expressing your emotions today?
- Today, how will you calm your mind and become focused?
- What is your spiritual practice for today? How will you enliven life?

❖❖❖❖

- Review your life for healing experiences.
- Can you recall a time when illness or injury opened you to new insights or emotions?
- Has your life ever been improved by living through emotional turmoil?
- Has a crisis of meaning ever deepened your spirituality?

Lesson 70

From Healing to Holy

There's no joy even in beautiful Wisdom, unless one has holy Health.

~ Simondes of Ceos

To the poet, to the philosopher, to the saint, all things are friendly and sacred, all events profitable, all days holy, all men divine.

~ Ralph Waldo Emerson

All of us are wounded and in need of healing. We are all broken at some level, and we struggle to be made whole. It is our life's journey.

We are wounded because no perfect families exist. No matter how hard our parents tried, all of us were disappointed or hurt by something. Some hurts were greater than others, but everyone has some childhood wounds. Other woundings come from a "lived" life. We all have had our breaking experiences where life fell apart. Sometimes it was bad luck, and other times we created the crisis by "acting out" our egocentric, self-centered nature. For many of us, it is true that we must be broken before we can open to life's potential for us. Only in brokenness do we awaken to our responsibility for the work of seeking wholeness.

Overcoming our brokenness and woundedness occurs through the process of healing. The words heal and healing comes from the Old English word *haelan*, which means to be made sound or whole. *Haelan* and its cousin *hai* are the root words for the modern English words of health, whole, and holy. The basic unfolding of life's journey is related to these words in this order: healing, healthy, whole, holy. All speak to the same fundamental process of psychological and spiritual growth toward the fulfillment of our purpose.

Healing is the process of coming into right relationship with body, mind, emotions, and spirit. It is finding the right balance in exercise, diet, mental challenges, emotional expression, and spiritual awareness. Healing leads us towards health. Health is that state when we are without symptoms, but our challenge is to go beyond health to wellness—to enhanced health. Ultimately, the healing journey is to wholeness with the integration of mind, body, and spirit.

As whole persons, we are brought into a relationship with that which is greater than us, as we recognize the limitations of the ego and connect to a "higher power." We come to understand our essential interconnectedness with all that surrounds us, from the smallest particle to the entire universe. As whole persons, we are called upon to take action and to nurture life in all its forms.

Eventually, as we move more deeply into right relationship, all the pieces of our life may fall into place, as we approach holiness. Holiness, sharing the same root as healing, health, and whole, is the experience of our full integration into who we were meant to be. *Holiness is where we live out our purpose.* In this state of right and holy relationship, we are deeply integrated within ourselves and can truly love and value who we are. We are empowered to love our neighbors in all their many forms as we reach out to them in loving kindness. We connected with a higher power that sustains creativity and courage in all these efforts. We become profoundly loving and, therefore, "holy" people.

The journey of life begins with loss. At our birth, we lose the security and safety of the womb as we emerge into the unknown. Life then takes us on a circuitous path where from our early wounds of separation, we go through stages of healing and health to approach wholeness with the potential of living in the holy moment. The holy moment is the ordinary moment—the present moment—when it is fully and consciously lived.

The journey towards wholeness is not straightforward. It is not once and for all. It is back and forth. We make progress, and then we lose ground. Overall, life's journey is a spiral-like process where we ever circle around and in toward the precious presence of a fully lived life. Obstacles are always encountered, and we can get stuck along the way. The successful journey of life must be mindfully taken with an intentional effort. It is a journey into ever growing consciousness and responsibility.

❖❖❖❖

- Where are you on the journey of life?
- Where are you in the process of healing?
- What is the state of your wellness?
- Are you becoming whole?
- Have you had holy moments?
- Do you know how to find them again?

Lessons to Come

L earn to look for awakening moments. While they are most readily perceived in moments of crisis, awakening moments surround us all the time. If we can open ourselves to a greater perception of possibility, they will become more readily visible.

Awakening moments always offer lessons. They help us to see the reality of what is before us and allow our common sense to provide insight into solutions for life's problems. Be alert for awakening moments, and when they occur, challenge yourself to change by putting your common sense into action.

❖❖❖

- Be aware.
- Be responsible.
- Evaluate options.
- Make a choice.
- Take action.
- See if life begins to go better.

Appendix A

Scoring for Depression Test

Scores of 1-10 Normal
Scores of 11-14 Normal Life Mood
Scores of 15-20 Headed Toward Depression
Scores of 21-25 Mild Depression
Scores of 26-30 Moderate Depression
Scores of Over 31 Severe Depression

If your score is in the mild, moderate, or severe range, you may want to talk to a counselor or your doctor.

❖❖❖❖

Appendix B

Awakenings Web Site Resources

The Awakenings Web site (http://www.lessons4living.com/) is a resource for additional information on *Simple Solutions for Life's Problems.*

- New *Lessons for Living* are frequently posted.
- Sign up for a free e-mail newsletter.
- Take on-line tests to assess stress, depression, or burnout.
- Unwind with on-line relaxation instructions.
- Download a relaxation sound file for your personal use.
- Download one of several free screen savers.
- Review Dr. Johnston's schedule of speaking engagements.

❖❖❖❖

Appendix C

Enjoyable Things List

Things You Like to Do	(W) Week	(P) Plan	(A) Alone	($) Money
1.				
2.				
3.				
4.				
5.				
6.				
7.				
8.				
9.				
10.				
11.				
12.				
13.				
14.				
15.				
16.				
17.				
18.				
19.				
20.				

References

Anderla, Georges. Study on the growth of knowledge reported by Peter Russell in *The White Hole in Time: Our Future Evolution and the Meaning of Now.* San Francisco: HarperSanFrancisco, 1992.

Benson, Herbert and Klipper, Miriam Z. (Contributor). *The Relaxation Response.* New York: Avon, 1990.

Boorstein, Sylvia. *It's Easier than You Think: The Buddhist Way to Happiness.* San Francisco: HarperSanFrancisco, 1997.

Butterworth, Eric. *Spiritual Economics: The Principles and Process of True Prosperity.* Unity Village, Missouri: Unity Books, 1997.

Campbell, Joseph. *The Power of Myth.* New York: Doubleday, 1988.

Ellis, Albert and Grieger, Russell. *Handbook of Rational-Emotive Therapy.* New York: Springer Publishing Company, 1977.

Nelson, Portia. *There is a Hole in My Sidewalk: The Romance of Self-Discovery.* Hillsboro, Oregon: Beyond Words Publishing, 1993.

Osbon, Diane, ed. *A Joseph Campbell Companion.* New York: HarperCollins Publisher, 1991.

Peck, Scott. *A World Waiting To Be Born.* New York: Bantam, 1993.

Sanford, John. Statement in an audio tape lecture.

Bonus Lesson

Reframing Your Mind

Could we change our attitude, we should not only see life differently, but life itself would come to be different. Life would undergo a change of appearance because we ourselves had undergone a change in attitude.

~ Katherine Mansfield

Have you ever reframed a picture? Perhaps one that did not go with your décor? You may have decorated in Danish Modern, but your artwork is in a frame style from the Italian Renaissance. It clashes with the room and is a distraction. Placing the same picture in a different and more suitable frame harmonizes and balances the atmosphere. The simple act of reframing leads to transformation in the room's appearance.

The concept of reframing is also found in psychology. It is to place a problem or situation into a new context of understanding. The new understanding changes the meaning of the situation, and a new meaning offers fresh possibilities To psychologically reframe something is to look at it from a different perspective. Most often this means from a new attitude.

A fundamental way of reframing anything is changing from a typically negative outlook to a more positive one. For example, you can reframe failure into opportunity. Thomas Edison, the inventor, did it all the time. In his effort to invent the light bulb he had 10,000 failures which he reframed as 10,000 ways that he had learned not to make a light bulb. Edison said, "I am not discouraged, because every wrong attempt discarded is another step forward." Failure became opportunity for Edison.

What can you reframe in your life? What new point of view can you wrap around a problem? When you are in a rush and caught by the traffic light, you can angrily think either, "This always happens" or, "Good, at last a moment to relax." When the rain cancels your picnic, you can complain about how "everything is ruined" or see it as the chance to visit the museum. When a relationship is in conflict, you can decide that it is over or see the possibility of working through to a deeper level of commitment. How about reframing:

- *It can't be done* into *It will be a challenge.*
- *It's no use* into *Let's try anyway.*
- *There's no hope* into *You never know what will happen.*

Learn to reframe your problems. Find a different framework. Look for one that is hopeful, optimistic, and energizing. Always look for other points of view, and choose one that works best for you. Redecorate and reframe your mind. See if life begins to go better.

❖❖❖❖

- Identify several of your problems.
- Can you rethink and reframe them?
- How do they look from a new perspective?

❖❖❖❖

*The willingness to accept responsibility for one's
own life is the source from which self-respect springs.*

~ Joan Didion

Order Form

Lessons for Living:
Simple Solutions for Life's Problems

Telephone orders: 478-471-1008

Mail orders: Dagali Press
5663 Taylor Terrace
Macon, GA 31210

Ship to:

Name_____

Address_____

City_____State_____Zip_____

Telephone_____

Please send:___ books at $11.95 Total = $_____
Shipping and handling
(Add $3.00 for first book,   = $ _____
 $.75 per additional book)

Total = $ _____

Dr. Johnston is available for lectures and workshops.

For information write   Dagali Press
5663 Taylor Terrace
Macon, Georgia 31210

Call: 478-471-1008
E-mail: dagalipress@lessons4living.com
Visit our Web Site: www.lessons4living.com

❖❖❖❖

Originality is the art of concealing your sources.

~ Horace Farfel

Order Form

Lessons for Living:
Simple Solutions for Life's Problems

Telephone orders: 478-471-1008

Mail orders: Dagali Press
                      5663 Taylor Terrace
                      Macon, GA 31210

Ship to:

Name_____

Address_____

City_____State_____Zip_____

Telephone_____

Please send:___ books at $11.95 Total = $_____
Shipping and handling
(Add $3.00 for first book,   = $ _____
 $.75 per additional book)
                      Total = $ _____

Dr. Johnston is available for lectures and workshops.

For information write   Dagali Press
                      5663 Taylor Terrace
                      Macon, Georgia 31210

Call: 478-471-1008
E-mail: dagalipress@lessons4living.com
Visit our Web Site: www.lessons4living.com

About the Author

Daniel H. Johnston, Ph.D. is a clinical psychologist and former Director of Psychological Services at the Medical Center of Central Georgia in Macon, Georgia. He serves on the faculty of the Mercer University School of Medicine. Over the past twenty-five years Dr. Johnston has taught self-help skills to thousands of people in settings ranging from hospitals and clinics to community groups and churches. He is a frequent guest on local television and has his own weekly show on 13WMAZ in Macon, Georgia.

Dr. Johnston has developed the popular Awakenings Web site (www.lessons4living.com) and offers information on psychological health to tens of thousands of worldwide visitors each year. He is a columnist for the Macon Telegraph newspaper and has also written a column for MyPrimeTime.com, a Web site that receives about three million visitors per month. Dr. Johnston has a current interest is in the use of labyrinths as tools for personal growth. He has helped build several labyrinths for local community use and has received a grant to build a labyrinth in a local area park located near several hospitals. Dr. Johnston serves on the Board of Directors of the International Labyrinth Society.